A. D. Cameron

Book One
From the Earliest Times to the Union of 1707

SECOND EDITION

Oliver & Boyd

Preface to the second edition

I welcome the decision to publish a new edition of this series using a wide variety of illustrations. For the sake of the many schools who find the books suited to their particular needs at present, the temptation to make changes for the sake of change has been firmly resisted. Content and coverage remain broadly the same as in the original edition of both books.

The opportunity has been taken to look again at topics from the stance of the late 1970s, taking account of changes in school organisation, recent historical works and recent events. Some parts have been rewritten to make them clearer and some new views and information have been incorporated, but the major change is the new collection of illustrations – maps, plans, drawings, paintings and photographs – which have been closely integrated with the text to provide inside each book a wide range of materials to help pupils to learn with pleasure.

I wish to thank very sincerely everyone who has helped with comments and information, and particularly in the search for interesting illustrations.

A.D.C.

Contents

1 People and Their Needs

There are more than five million of us in Scotland to-day, living mainly in towns. While some of the towns are far apart, such as Thurso and Dumfries, or Oban and Aberdeen, most of them are in the central Lowlands, between the Highlands of the north and the Uplands of the south. They have grown up there, many in the last two centuries, because of the coal underneath them.

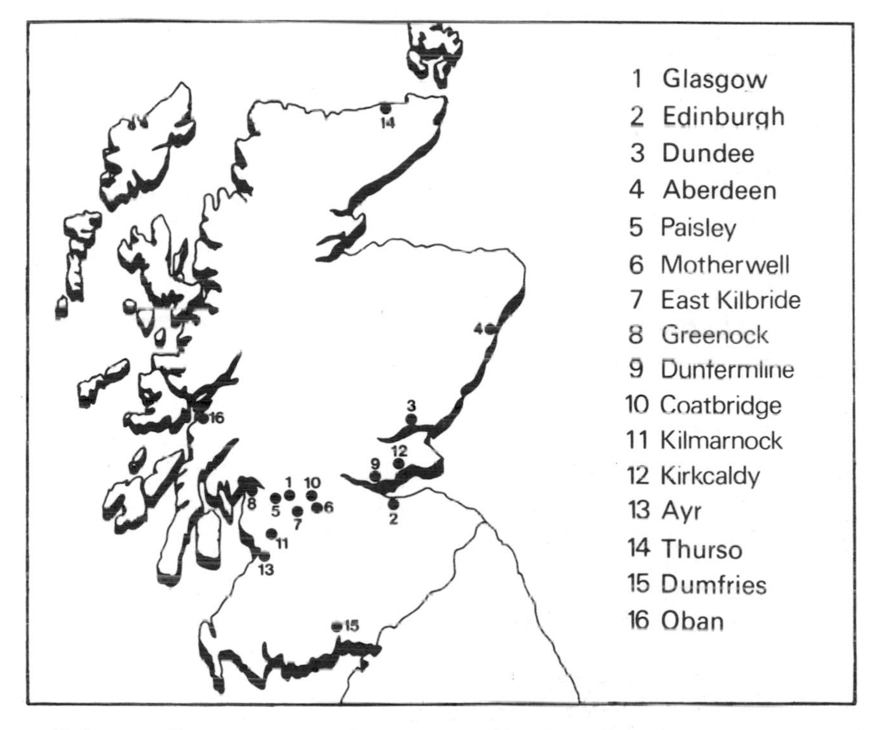

Most of you attend town schools. Your parents and brothers and sisters may work in factories, workshops, shipyards or mines, *producing* things; or drive lorries or vans, *transporting* things from place to place, or in offices and shops, taking orders and *selling* things. All these jobs are connected, and are necessary to support our modern lives.

A man in a shipyard is not building a boat because he wants it for himself. He works there because a shipping company has placed an order for a ship, and with hundreds of others he helps to make it. In return for his work he receives a wage in money which he uses to provide for the needs of his family.

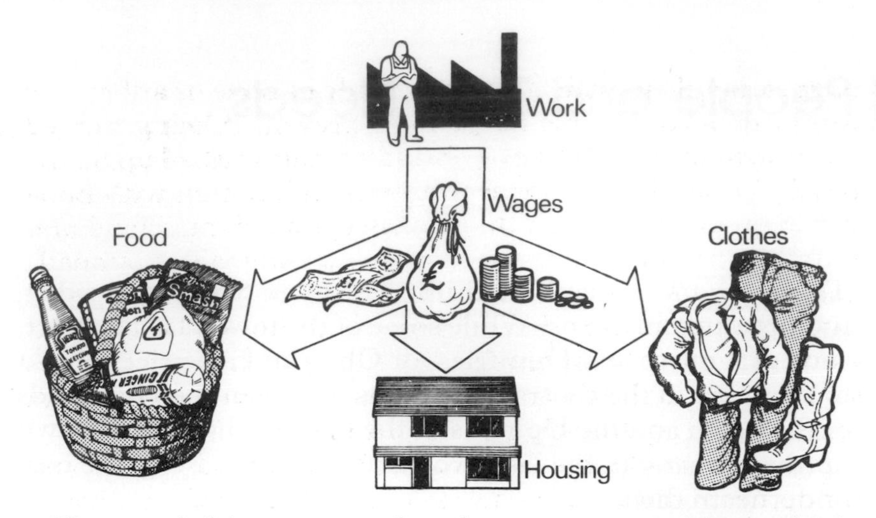

He spends his money as he pleases on some things which his family need, and on other things which, though not absolutely necessary, they happen to like. There are three basic things we need to keep us alive.

1. We need *food and drink*.
2. We need *shelter*, usually some kind of house, to protect us from the weather and to allow us to live our lives in our own way.
3. We need *clothes* to keep us warm and dry when we are out in the open.

Probably you can think of many other things which you feel you need, but these three, food, shelter and clothing, are our basic or *economic* needs. Without them we could not live.

Today, working at one job, earning a wage and spending it in his own way, a man can keep himself alive without growing all his own food, building his own house or making his own clothes.

It has not always been like this.

In early Scotland

Imagine yourself on a deserted island. You are between the sea and the unexplored forest. You begin to feel hungry and think about food. You must look for it. You are in the same position as the earliest man in Scotland, who arrived in Fife as early as 5500 BC. He was a food-gatherer. He had most chance of survival on the seashore, where he gathered shellfish. We know this from rubbish heaps full of shells found on or near the shore. At the right seasons he picked berries, and in the forest he collected nuts.

To get food at other times, he learned to fish and hunt. He caught fish with his hands, or by stunning them with a stone or spearing them with a harpoon made of bone or antler. He would tie a cord to his harpoon to prevent it being carried away downstream. If he ever found a whale washed up on the beach, he and his friends would hack off its flesh with bone cutting tools. Except on the windswept north mainland and islands, Scotland was covered by trees. Animals abounded: giant deer, elk, wild oxen, wolves, beavers, lemmings, wild cats, mountain hares, boars, ponies and brown bears. Man learned to make weapons for hunting. Often he was not as strong as the animals he hunted, and he went hunting with other men. Together they made pits to trap animals.

If you strike a piece of flint on a stone you make sparks, and if you use dried moss or fungus or rotten wood or thistle-down as tinder, it will smoulder and burst into flame. You have started a fire with a 'strike-a-light'. Another way of making a fire was by rubbing wood against wood in the Boy Scout manner. A piece of wood with grooves in it was placed on the ground and a round piece of wood was rubbed vigorously in a groove until the friction made dust and the heat caused the dust to smoulder and catch fire. Making fire in either of these ways was not easy, and when people had a fire going they tried to make sure it never went out.

This discovery completely altered the life of man. People could keep themselves warm, cook their food instead of eating it raw, and ward off wild animals at night. Later they learned to work metals and make weapons by the heat of a fire.

After scraping the skins of animals on the inside with a sharp stone, they sewed them into clothes. By rubbing bones down, they made needles for sewing and harpoons for hunting and fishing.

Where there were caves they sheltered in them. In most places they probably lived in tents of skins, the first man-made homes in Scotland.

No sign of these tent-like dwellings can be seen now, but they are the kind of homes we should expect a hunting people to use (compare the tepees of Red Indians). The only traces these people have left are solid things like stone, bone and pottery made of fired clay, while later people have left their metal tools and weapons. But wood, bark, leather and, later, cloth, must have been just as important in the daily lives of early peoples. From bark alone they could have made baskets and boxes, cradles, shoes, torches, handles for tools and roofs for houses. We cannot find any traces of these now to help us to learn the full story of the people who used them.

Something for You to Do

1. *a*) Is your town marked on the map?
   b) What is its name?
   c) How many people live in it?
2. The number of people living in Glasgow, Edinburgh and Aberdeen adds up to over one and a half million. What fraction of the population of Scotland lives in these three towns?
3. What do most people work at in your town?
4. Name the three groups in the second paragraph of this chapter into which most jobs are divided. In which group does your father's or mother's, brother's or sister's job belong?
5. We need food, shelter and clothing to keep us alive. What other things do you feel you need to make life enjoyable?
6. *a*) What kinds of berries and nuts which we can eat grow wild today?
   b) Which animals run wild in the countryside now?
7. *a*) What different ways can you strike a light today?
   b) Which people at the present day use the old methods?
8. On a double page of your notebook start off a chart with the headings given below:

	People	Food	Shelter	Clothing
1	Early Man			

Fill in how early man satisfied his needs. As you read the next three chapters you can add what you learn about later peoples.

2 The First Farmers

It was in the Near East that men made so much progress that they could be considered civilised. Before 3500 BC good crops of grain and flax were being raised on the mud-flats of the Nile delta in Egypt. Farther up the river, trenches were dug to carry water to the fields. When the ox-drawn plough was introduced it became possible to grow much more food with far less labour. Egypt became prosperous under the rule of kings called Pharaohs. The royal officials collected taxes and made people obey the laws. Under them a huge force of labourers controlled the River Nile and made canals, while others erected public buildings and tombs. The Great Pyramid, for example, a royal tomb, is thought to have taken a hundred thousand men about twenty years to build.

At about the same time, settlers were attracted to Mesopotamia, the land between the two great rivers, Tigris and Euphrates, which flow into the Persian Gulf. In addition to growing crops, people kept cows for milk and made cloth from the wool of their sheep. Their rulers had well-equipped and disciplined soldiers, some of whom charged into battle in chariots. Silver money was introduced, and people began to buy and sell goods instead of exchanging one article for another. The value of the money depended on its weight. Skilful smiths made beautiful ornaments from other metals, including gold and copper.

In both Egypt and Mesopotamia people could write. In Egypt they wrote on paper which they made from strips of river reed called papyrus, and in Mesopotamia they cut out the letters on tablets of wet clay. Both civilisations produced a calendar, showing that they could measure time. The Egyptian calendar was the more accurate. It divided the year into twelve months of thirty days each, with five feast days at the end to make a total of 365 days. These are some of the ways in which the peoples of the Near East were further advanced than those in Europe.

New Stone Age People in Scotland

About 3500 BC new people began to settle in Scotland. They came from the shores of south-west Europe in boats

How the New Stone Age people came to Scotland

hollowed out of tree trunks. They came gradually, hugging the coast, some settling in the south and east of England. Many perished on the way, but the most skilful and the strongest survived. By way of the Irish Sea they reached the western mainland and islands and settled, while some went farther north to settle in the Shetland Isles. The east coast was settled, too, when the descendants of the people who had made their homes in south-east England came north by sea. We do not know what race they were, because they left no written records. But we know something of their way of life from the materials they used for the best of their weapons, and we call them New Stone Age people.

These people were better equipped to obtain their basic needs than the earlier food-gatherers and primitive hunters had been. They had tamed dogs to help them in hunting. They had axes of polished stone, shaped and smoothed. Their cutting and boring tools, however, were not like modern tools, because they did not know how to use metals. If you look at the time chart at the back of this book, you will see that before 3500 BC people elsewhere were already using copper. In Scotland at this time men took lumps of hard stone called *flint*, and split them into flakes.

They made knives, borers, scrapers, daggers and arrowheads out of flakes, which they sharpened by striking them on the edge with a hammer stone. Among the weapons they used were the bow and arrow. The shaft of the arrow was shaved smooth with a flint knife and scraper, the tail was trimmed with feathers from a bird like the eagle or the goose, and in the head a piece of flint was fixed. The earliest arrowheads were shaped like a birch or a willow leaf.

If you think that stone tools were not much use you are wrong. Not long ago a worker in Denmark was given stone tools instead of steel ones. He cut wood, made planks and built a complete house with them by himself in less than twelve weeks.

Living at Skara Brae

Let us take a close-up view of the New Stone Age folk who lived at Skara Brae in Orkney five thousand years ago.

On the sandy shore of the Bay of Skaill on the west coast of Orkney a whale has been cast up by the sea. Men are hacking off chunks of flesh which their womenfolk pile into big whalebone basins. Children chase one another round and over the top of this mountain of flesh. Everyone is chattering,' Here is food; here is plenty.' The cattle and the sheep are left unguarded on the pastures. No one is hunting for seabirds today and no one is out fishing for cod.

An old man sits on a stone to rest.

'The sea has been good to us,' he murmurs. 'Now no one need starve. There is food here for many moons. Look at

Inside a hut at Skara Brae today

these huge bones. Why, we can make new supports for our roofs.' He points towards a jumble of connected domes where smoke rises. 'We can make more basins to hold water and milk. Our women will be pleased to have new awls to sew together our clothes of skin. They can boil the blubber and get plenty of oil for cooking. This big skin would make clothes for all of us, but we shall use it to re-roof our houses to keep the rain out. Yes, the sea has been kind.' He picks up his knife of split beach-pebble and returns to help the excited, toiling men.

When they are tired from their labours, they carry the flesh, the blubber, the bones and the skin towards the rising smoke. They seem to be walking into the side of a hill. Perhaps all these people live in the ground. No, they have built their houses at Skara Brae very cunningly. On the ground they have carefully laid flat slabs of stone, and piled more stones on top of them to make square rooms, with the walls sloping slightly inward. As the winds from the sea can blow through walls built without mortar and make the houses cold and draughty, the people pile their rubbish outside the walls until the spaces between the eight huts are almost completely filled in. To go from one house to another they creep along low covered alleys. They may be living in their own midden but they do keep the heat in and the strong winds out.

To enter their huts they have to keep their heads down. Inside, they dump their loads of flesh beside the hearth in the middle of the room, where the peat fire is burning low. The mother sets to work attending to the fire, filling up her cooking pot and setting it to boil. Soon they are sitting on their beds, eating their supper of stew. It all seems strange to us, but this is their home and now they are happy in it. Their single room is roughly six or seven paces across. (You can compare this with the size of your classroom or a room at home.) Whalebones form the rafters for the roof of whaleskin, and there may be a hole in the roof to let smoke out.

All the furniture is made of stone, because few trees grow on the islands. At each side of the fire, at floor level, is a bed like a box of stone with a canopy of skins over it. In these box-beds the people sleep on heather and dried grass, covering themselves with skins. At one end of the room stands a dresser made of stone, holding pots and basins on its shelves. There, and in little cupboards in the walls, the people keep their belongings.

They made themselves beads and dice from bones and from the ivory tusks of the walrus. In one of the houses at Skara Brae, the smaller bed (almost certainly a woman's) contained beads and also pots with colour in them, which suggests that they decorated themselves—no recent custom this! Animal bones found in the beds tell us that the family chewed the meat from them in bed.

Theirs were peaceful lives and they had no weapons of war.

What the inside of a hut at Skara Brae might have been like in the New Stone Age

It was no human enemy that turned out the folk of Skara Brae, but the sea and sand sweeping in. They left in a hurry, leaving everything as it was, even the beads from a necklace which snapped as someone scurried along the passageway to safety.

The settlement of Skara Brae disappeared under a blanket of sand. Now archaeologists, who 'dig for history', have rediscovered it and revealed a clear picture of life in Orkney so many years ago.

Farming

If a hunter is unsuccessful he has nothing to eat. The New Stone Age settlers from Europe, however, had learned to *domesticate*, or tame, animals, and they brought cattle and sheep with them. The list on page 7 shows you that sheep were not native to this country. People now hunted less, for their herds of cattle and sheep made their supply of milk and meat more reliable. It was difficult to keep animals during the cold winter months. Many were killed in autumn. The others were fed on hay, twigs and leaves, seaweed, whalemeat and bark, chopped up and boiled in water. Meat was hung up to dry in the wind to help to cure it.

Stone axes and tools of flint made it easier to cut down trees. Men used to fear the forests, which were dark and full of wild animals, but gradually they conquered them and made the trees useful friends. Wood was valuable for building huts and boats. Often the trees were felled and burned to encourage fresh grass to grow for feeding the herds and to provide new land for growing grain. Men either scattered their seeds and raked them among the wood ash, or they made holes with a stick, put in barley seeds and covered them with soil. They made sickles for harvesting by using pitch to fix a row of sharp flints into a wooden handle, and they cut the barley stalks not far below the heads. The best seeds from the year's harvest were kept for sowing the next year.

Grinding corn

You may wonder how we know that these people grew barley. Several jars known to have been made in the New Stone Age have marks of barley seeds on them. The seeds must have become embedded in the clay when it was still wet.

People, probably the women, spent about an hour every day grinding the corn into flour by working a rubbing stone backwards and forwards on a big smooth stone called a quern. After mixing the flour with water or milk, they baked bread or cakes on stones warmed by the heat of the fire.

The soil became exhausted after growing crops for three or four years in a row. The people would have to clear new ground and might have to move on, but they were becoming *settlers* rather than wanderers. Growing crops meant a more certain and better food supply, which in turn meant that fewer people starved and the population increased.

We should not think that the New Stone Age people were very poor and uncivilised. Certainly their needs were simple, but they must have produced enough food to allow some men, such as stone masons, to do specialised jobs. The magnificent burial mound of Maeshowe in Orkney, for example, must have been built by a big number of skilled craftsmen. They handled stones weighing as much as three tonnes, and built dry-stone walls so carefully that the edges of the stones fitted exactly into one another. Here some great chief and his family were buried.

Something for You to Do

1. *a*) Write down the date when New Stone Age people began to land in Scotland.
   b) Beneath it, write this year's date.
   c) How many years ago did the first New Stone Age people come?
2. Try to find out more about what the people in the early civilisations in Egypt and Mesopotamia could do.
3. *a*) Make a list of the tools and weapons made from flint.
   b) Opposite each one, write down what it would be used for
4. What do you think were the three greatest discoveries made in the New Stone Age?
5. *a*) In the picture on page 12 find a bed, the dresser, the hearth and a wall cupboard.
   b) Why did the people of Skara Brae use stone furniture?
   c) Why did they leave their homes?
   d) Draw a plan or make a model of the inside of a Skara Brae house.
6. Add to your chart on food, shelter and clothing what you have learned about people in the New Stone Age.
7. *The Boy with the Bronze Axe* by Kathleen Fidler is a story about young people living in Skara Brae just before it was buried in the sand.

3 Makers of Bronze, Weavers of Cloth

Left on their own, the New Stone Age farmers would have had to wait a long time before one of them discovered metals. While they were working with stone tools, people in lands round the Mediterranean Sea, such as Egypt, had learned to mine copper and smelt it and make tools out of it. Then about 3000 BC, someone in Europe discovered that when a small quantity of tin was added to copper and heated, bronze, a harder metal, was formed. The *Bronze Age* had begun. We still use bronze at the present day. Look in your pockets and see if you have any 'coppers'. Pence are made of bronze.

In the time chart at the end of this book you will see that the Bronze Age lasted for a long, long time—about fifteen hundred years. Metal came in gradually but it was not used everywhere, or for everything. Stone axes, for example, were still very useful and men still found that flint made good arrowheads. Later, as the land became more crowded, the weapons men had hunted with began to be used in war.

It was from Ireland that people here first learned about metals. Ireland had good supplies of gold and copper and some men became skilful metal-workers. They made weapons and tools of bronze which were carried across the sea to be traded with people in Scotland.

Bronze Age Homes

The first settlers to come to Scotland knowing how to work metals we call the Beaker people. They came over to the British Isles including Ireland from Germany and the Low Countries. Very few signs of their homes have been found here and we do not know enough about their lives. We know them rather from the way they buried their dead, usually in little coffins with sides of flat stones and a huge stone cover on top. With the body they would put a flint knife or a flint arrowhead, perhaps, and sometimes a decorated clay pot called a beaker, probably filled with drink for the journey to the next world.

In the village of Jarlshof, in the south of Shetland, some people lived in four oval houses which they had built solidly with stones. When he entered a house, a stranger found

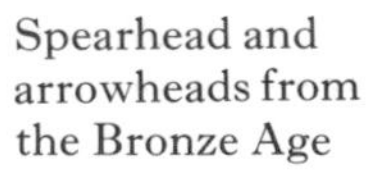

Spearhead and arrowheads from the Bronze Age

Bronze Age jewellery:
(left) gold crescent
(right) jet necklace

himself in a central room where a peat fire burned. On each side he could see into the little round cubicles (the other rooms) which had walls and roofs of stone. Cattle were kept in the largest room at the far end. Whether or not a hole was left in the roof to let the smoke out, is anyone's guess.

Later on, perhaps about 700 BC, a bronze-smith set up his smithy in a room inside the entrance to one of these houses. Using clay moulds he cast axes and swords. The weapons were exactly like those the smiths in Ireland made. He must have settled down to work at his trade among the people of Jarlshof. Few craftsmen can have worked under greater handicaps, for tin had to be imported from Cornwall and charcoal for the furnace from the mainland, except when enough driftwood was cast up on the shore.

Another Bronze Age house, at Muirkirk in Ayrshire, was a stone circle measuring ten and a half metres across. The wall was low and thick. In the centre, the trunk of an oak tree held up the roof. Here, too, the people and their animals lived in the same building.

Women's Work

When the women were not cooking or grinding barley they might make their own pottery and cloth. Using clay, they produced many of the things they needed in the home: pots and bowls for cooking and keeping food, ladles and spinning whorls. They shaped the clay with their hands and cooked it in an oven until it was hard.

Weaving and spinning

They made cloth from wool. After plucking the wool from the sheep, they combed it. Then the wool was spun, that is, twisted to give it strength. A woman held the raw wool wrapped on a stick called a distaff. She pulled out a length of wool and attached it to a stick which had a whorl as a weight on the end. She held this in her other hand, and by twisting the stick spun the yarn. Then the yarn was woven into cloth on a simple loom.

In some places blue-petalled flax was grown and harvested to be made into linen. Dyes from plants and berries allowed the cloth to be coloured. For the first time people were wearing clothes which were not made of skin.

Something for You to Do

1. Bronze:
   a) Which two metals are used to make it?
   b) Why does bronze make better weapons than copper?
   c) What difficulties did the bronze-smith face in Jarlshof?
2. Do the pictures about Bronze Age people make you think they were warlike or civilised, and why?
3. Add to your chart on food, shelter and clothing what you have learned about the people in the Bronze Age.
4. The book *Warrior Scarlet* by Rosemary Sutcliff will tell you more about life in the Bronze Age.

4 The Iron Age Celts

When the first Celts arrived about 700 BC, they were armed with swords and axes of bronze. Later Celts had iron weapons. Some came north overland while others left the north of England by sea and landed on the banks of the Tweed, Forth and Tay.

They were fierce conquerors, organised in tribes. Their warriors loved fighting and kept a record of the number of men they killed. The ornaments they wore, the decorated trappings on their horses and the quality of their weapons were all signs that these men were proud of their skill in war. Led by their chiefs, they rode in chariots, which were as fearsome in battle then as the tank is today. Their priests, the Druids, were looked up to because they were the guardians of the law, poets and advisers to the chiefs. The Celts conquered the local people, whom they forced to work for them.

Many of the farmers had lived in undefended farmsteads, but the unsettled times forced them to build wooden fences to protect themselves. People began to look for safety in high places or behind stone walls. Their settlements became not simply houses to live in and four different kinds of defended places have been found:

1. Hilltop forts
2. Hilltop villages
3. Brochs
4. Crannogs.

1. Hilltop Forts

A hilltop fort with thick walls of wood and stone

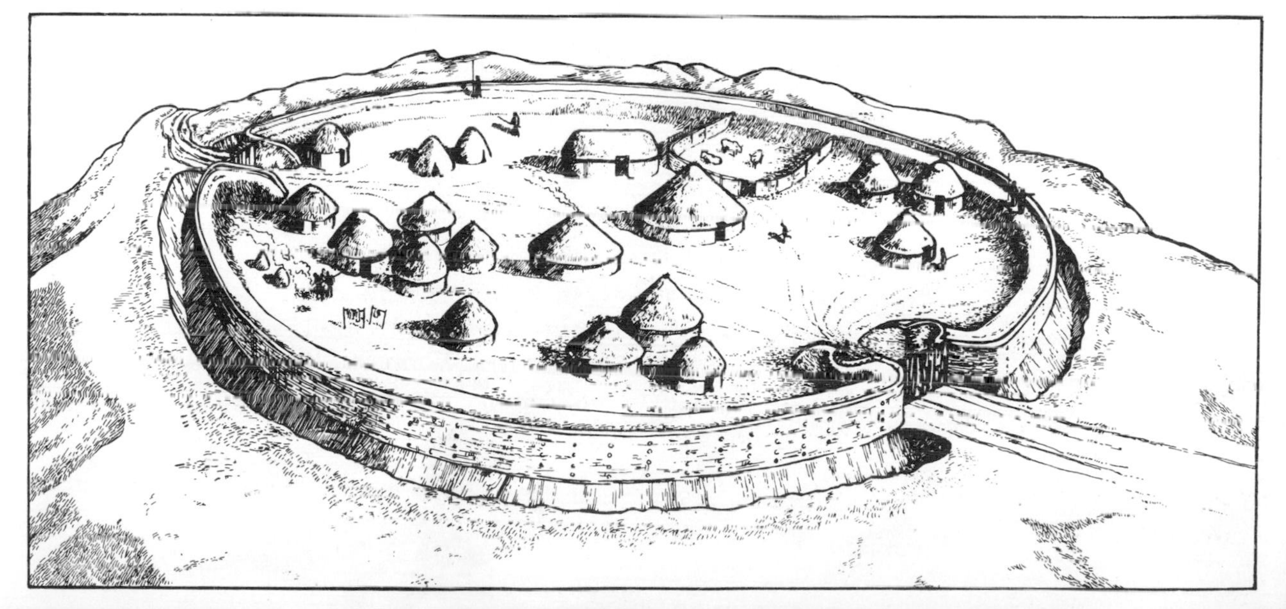

Between Inverness and the Tay, early forts on hilltops were defended by walls of stone constructed on a framework of wood. The rampart of the fort at Finavon in Angus was over three and a half metres high and nearly twice as wide, stretching for nearly 300 metres round the hilltop. Inside the walls people's houses were round wooden huts on foundations of stone and turf. In Gaul [France] later, forts like these were named 'Gallic forts' by Julius Caesar.

2. Hilltop Villages

In the south-east also the people lived in villages on hilltops, or at least above the arable land. Traprain Law (east of Edinburgh) was an important tribal capital. It covered an area of thirteen hectares, big enough for it to be called a town. The walls of the round houses were made of wattle and daub, that is, they had a framework of interlaced sticks plastered with clay or mud. The folk there lived by farming and making things. They trained oxen to pull the plough, and prodded them along with sticks with iron tips called goads. The first evidence of a plough has been found at Blackburn Mill in Berwickshire. The people made and wore woollen clothes. Glass armlets, bronze dress fasteners, pins, brooches and mountings for harness were all made by craftsmen in the town. These ornaments, and also wool and cloth, were traded with other tribes.

3. Brochs *(1st century BC)*

The Broch of Mousa, Shetland

Inside a broch

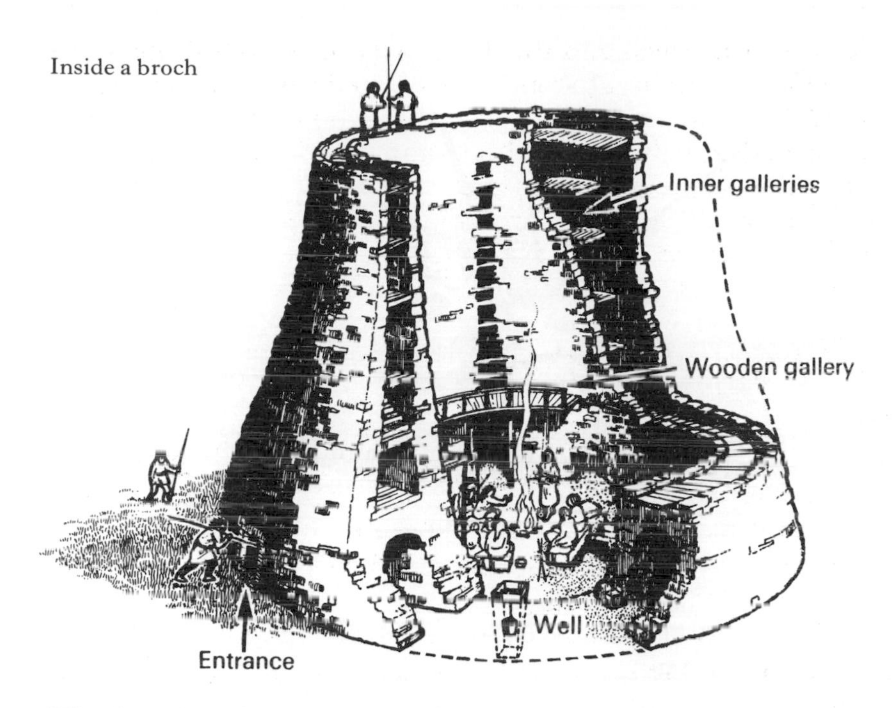

The brochs of the north and west were the biggest and most imposing buildings in Scotland before the Middle Ages, and are not found in any other country in Europe. They were great round towers with massive walls of unmortared stones. The entrance was a low tunnel which could be blocked by a stone door. The central courtyard, with a well and an open fireplace, was the scene of day-to-day life and work. It was partly covered over, above head-level, by a lean-to roof, held up by wooden posts. People slept and kept their belongings in little rooms on the ground, or up a stair inside the walls. Inside the broch, they were safe from their enemies. Nobody could climb up the sheer, solid walls and they were too thick to be shattered by a battering-ram.

The broch men very often built near the sea or a river, and always on good farming land. They had learned that a field left fallow and used as pasture for animals would soon recover its strength and produce good crops.

4. Crannogs

Just as some of the Celts looked for safety on hilltops, others, especially in Ayrshire and Galloway, used surrounding water to protect them. In some lochs, they lived on natural islands. More often the islands were man-made, and on each a hut or cluster of huts was erected. These are called crannogs or lake dwellings.

A crannog. Notice how they reached home safely

Great wooden uprights were driven into the bed of the loch to give the artificial island its main supports. The uprights were connected by flat beams of oak, through which they fitted like mortised joints. Within this framework layer upon layer of stones, branches of trees, tree trunks and brushwood was placed to raise the island safely above the level of the water. Wooden huts were built on this foundation. At Milton Loch, west of Dumfries, the house was round, walled with logs and thatched with rushes. On the platform round the house the men dried their nets. The fire was inside the house on a hearth of flat stones.

The people had to reach their island homes but try to prevent their enemies from doing so. Usually they made canoes from hollowed-out tree trunks about six metres long and over half a metre deep. Sometimes they made a zig-zagging road under the water, by which a native who knew the way could wade to and from the shore. At Milton Loch, there was a paved causeway.

People in the Iron Age

Iron began to replace bronze, not because it made better tools or weapons but because it was easier to produce and much cheaper. With plenty of farm implements like ploughs, hoes and sickles made of iron, land was cultivated more easily and more of the forest was cleared for farming.

Other materials were still used: bone for combs and needles, and for dice for playing a game; stone for pot lids, spinning whorls, querns and lamps; and bronze for jewellery.

You will notice that Scotland was not united. Many different families and tribes occupied it. Although they built different kinds of homes, they all lived by keeping herds and growing crops. Their chariots (showing their knowledge of the wheel), their pottery and their ornaments, demonstrate that they were not uncivilised, although they were less civilised than the next invaders, the Romans.

Something for You to Do

1. Write a paragraph describing the Celts preparing for battle.
2. *a*) On a map of Scotland show where each of the four kinds of Iron Age settlements were most common.
   b) Draw the kind of settlement that was common in your district, and try to collect information and pictures about it.
3. Under the heading of *Traprain Law* make a list of the things made and used there which show that the people were civilised.
4. *The Stronghold* by Mollie Hunter is a story about the broch-builders.
5. Add to your chart on food, shelter and clothing what you have learned about the people of the Iron Age.

A Celtic warrior in his chariot

5 The Romans Come and Conquer

The last great Mediterranean civilisation was that of Rome. Having conquered the Latin farmers of central Italy, the Romans gained control of the whole country. Carthage, a trading city across the sea in North Africa, challenged the Romans, and her soldiers under Hannibal crossed the Alps and advanced almost to the gates of Rome. But the Romans recovered, and wiped out the city of Carthage. During the two centuries before Christ, the Roman legions marched and fought and conquered all the lands round their sea, which they called *Mediterranean*, 'The Sea in the Middle of the Land'.

What a Roman legionary looked like

Julius Caesar

The great general Julius Caesar conquered Gaul [France]. From it he sighted this land, which he called *Britannia*, 'The Land of the Britons'. His two invasions, in 55 and 54 BC which first brought Britain into recorded history, were not successful, but they did tell the Britons that Rome existed and was strong.

Not long afterwards, Rome became an Empire under Caesar's nephew, Augustus, who was ruler over Judea when Jesus was born. Nowadays, when we wish to give the date of an event, we say that it took place a certain number of years *before* or *after* the birth of Christ. The letters 'BC' beside a date, stand for the words 'Before Christ'. The letters 'AD' mean 'After Christ'. They really stand for two Latin words, *Anno Domini* which mean 'In the Year of our Lord'. So when we say '50 BC', we mean 'fifty years *before* Christ was born', and when we say 'AD 50', we mean 'fifty years *after* Christ was born'.

The Roman Conquest of Britain

The serious conquest of Britain began in AD 43 when the Emperor Claudius sent legions to these shores. The south and east of the country were taken only with difficulty and, while the Romans were trying to conquer the tribes of north Wales, Boadicea, the queen of the tribe of Iceni in the east, led her people in revolt. They recaptured London, burned the town and killed thousands of Romans. The revolt was crushed, and then the Romans pushed on westwards and northwards.

Agricola

Julius Agricola proved to be a wise ruler and a skilful general when he became governor of Roman Britain.

Once he had conquered the people in the north of Wales, southern Britain became settled. At each of the three big Roman fortresses, York, Chester and Caerleon-on-Usk, a legion of crack troops was stationed, and they built long, straight roads to allow them to move quickly to any trouble-spot. Legionaries from York, for example, could march north along Dere Street to deal with raids by the tribes in the north. South and east of a line between these three fortresses, Britain prospered under Roman rule.

Where there were soldiers, there was money, and where there was money, trade. Garrison towns attracted traders, and towns grew up at river crossings, such as London, and at places where roads crossed, such as Lincoln. The Roman farm was called a *villa*, and was a large range of buildings, including barracks for the labourers. British landowners built villas like these, and increased their output of food so much that they were able to feed the townsfolk and the Roman soldiers. New vegetables such as the cabbage, the beetroot and the pea were introduced, and fruit trees such as the cherry. British chiefs began to wear the toga, and their sons learned to write Latin. They paid taxes to the Romans, and benefited from *Pax Romana*, or the 'Roman Peace'.

The Romans in Scotland

About AD 80, Roman legions crossed the Cheviots into *Caledonia*, as they called Scotland, and Agricola built a line of temporary forts between the firths of Forth and Clyde. North of the Tay, he established more forts including the great fort at Inchtuthil, which was big enough for an entire legion of 5000 men. From this base he tried to conquer the North. Some of the hilltop forts are now called *vitrified forts* because their timber-framed stone walls were burned with such intense heat that the material 'ran together'. The burning used to be blamed on the Romans but we now know that some were burned long before the Romans came.

The Celts saw nothing of Roman civilisation, only the damage the Roman soldiers did. 'They make a wilderness and they call it peace,' said Calgacus, a Celtic chief.

In AD 84, Agricola fell on the northern tribes at the battle of *Mons Graupius*. Many of the Celts were killed and the rest driven into the hills. Before Agricola could try to invade the Highlands, however, he was recalled to Rome. But he had made Scotland, south of the Forth and Clyde, part of the Roman Empire.

Later the raiding Celts from the north forced the Romans to withdraw from Scotland altogether. A line between the Solway Firth and the Tyne was chosen by the Emperor Hadrian for building a wall, which was to be the northern limit of the Roman Empire.

The Romans in Scotland

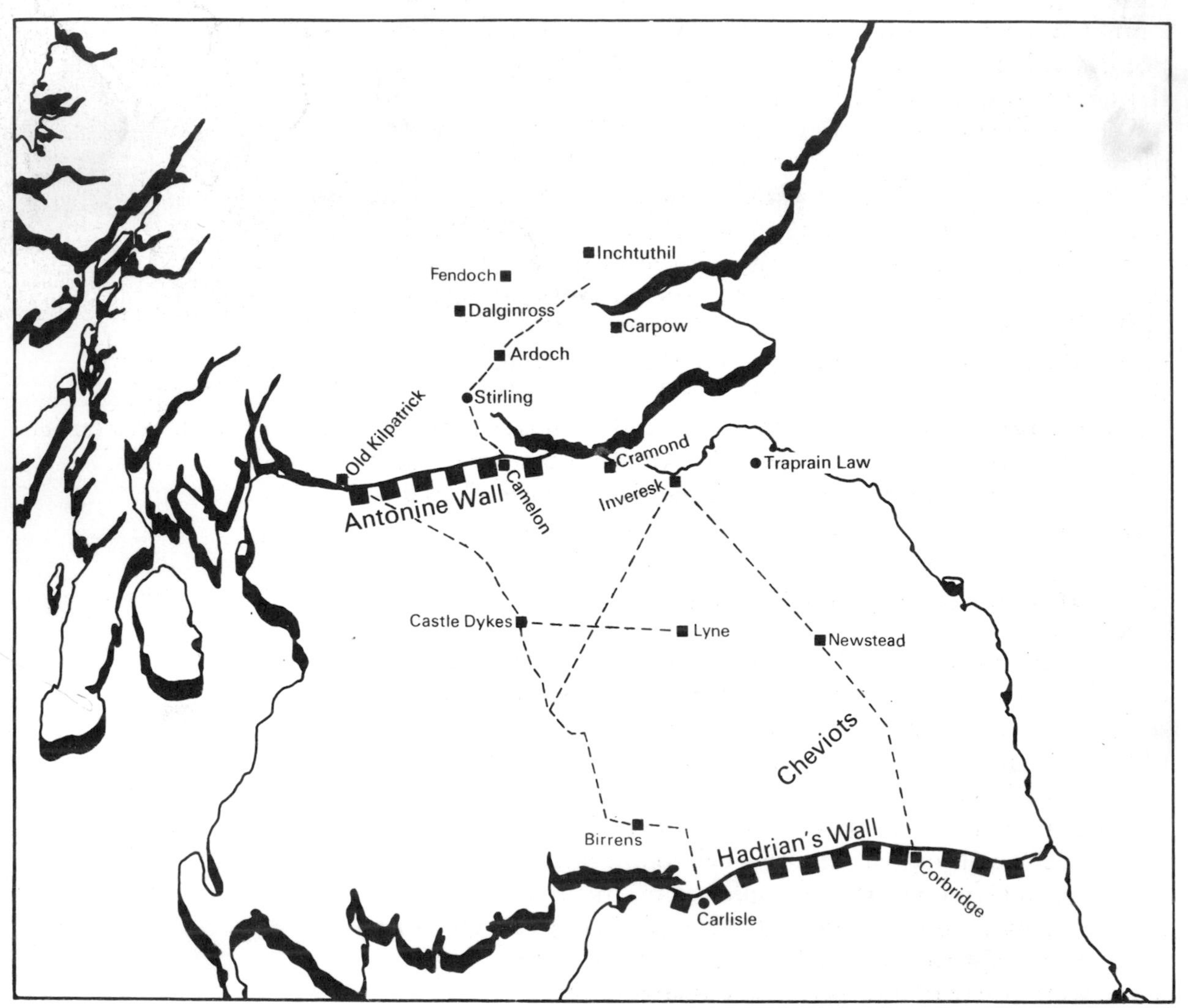

Hadrian's Wall, with its turrets and milecastles, and road running behind it (reconstruction by Alan Sorrell)

Hadrian's Wall

As it stands today, this wall is by far the largest and most spectacular historical ruin in Britain. It stretches more than one hundred and twelve kilometres from sea to sea. On the north side of it is a deep ditch, and behind it runs a straight road connecting the forts. Built by the Roman soldiers between AD 122 and 128, the wall is two and a half metres wide, faced with dressed stones on either side, and filled in with rubble between the stone blocks. The picture above shows it as it used to be with its walls over four metres high.

Along the wall were a series of strong forts, on the same pattern as Newstead[1] but smaller in size, each being able to house from 500 to 1 000 men. Between them, every 1 000 paces, were 'milecastles', where guards looked out constantly over the bleak moorland for signs of Celts on a raid. The soldiers who manned the wall were not legionaries, but *auxiliaries* recruited from tribes all over the Empire: among them were Belgians, Germans and Spaniards.

[1] See next chapter.

A story in stone from the eastern end of the Antonine Wall

The Antonine Wall

In AD 142, the Romans occupied the south of Scotland again, and, as Agricola had done earlier, they chose the narrowest part between the Clyde and the Forth as the new frontier. Here they built a new boundary. It was just over half the length of Hadrian's Wall, running for sixty kilometres from sea to sea. In front was a ditch, three and a half metres deep and twelve metres wide. Six metres behind it they laid a foundation of stones, and built square blocks of turf into a huge mound, four and a half metres at the base, three and a half metres high and nearly two metres wide at the top. The legionaries did all the work. One of their inscriptions reads: 'In honour of the Emperor...Antoninus Augustus Pius, father of his country, the Second Legion, Augustus's own, completed [the work of the wall] for 4652 paces'.

At intervals along the wall were nineteen forts, roughly one every three kilometres, and soldiers could move easily from one fort to another along the military road behind it. Auxiliary soldiers manned these forts.

Something for You to Do

1. Which three towns in Roman Britain had legions stationed in them?
2. List the ways in which the people in the south of Britain benefited from the presence of the Romans.
3. Make a map of Roman Scotland showing Hadrian's Wall, the Antonine Wall, Newstead, Inchtuthil, Cramond and the Roman roads.
4. At Inchtuthil in the 1960s archaeologists discovered about a million iron nails. They were covered by nearly two metres of clay. They were different sizes, seven and a half centimetres up to thirty centimetres long, and all of high quality iron.
   a) What does this tell us about the material used to build Inchtuthil and other forts in the north?
   b) The Romans buried them deep to hide them from the natives. What might their enemies make out of 10 tonnes of good iron?
5. 'Roman Wall Blues' by W. H. Auden is a poem on how a soldier felt about being a sentry on the wall.
6. For more about the Romans, see *The Romans in Britain* by Dorothy Morrison in Oliver & Boyd's *Exploring History* series.

6 The Roman Soldiers at Newstead

Agricola chose a good position below the three hills which gave the fort its name, *Trimontium* (now Newstead). It commanded the crossing of the River Tweed to the north of it and stood about half-way between the Tyne and the Forth. The fort, covering an area of six hectares, was the usual shape, square with rounded corners. It had a massive rampart round it, with a stone wall on top, and deep ditches outside it. Outside were other camps and on one of the hills a signal station.

Within the defences, the buildings were laid out as the drawing shows. In the centre were the headquarters of the fort, where the standards and pay-chests were kept. On one side was the commandant's house, and on the other the officers' quarters. The commandant's house was centrally heated by a hypocaust, a fire from which hot air passed under

The Roman fort at Newstead (reconstruction by Alan Sorrell)

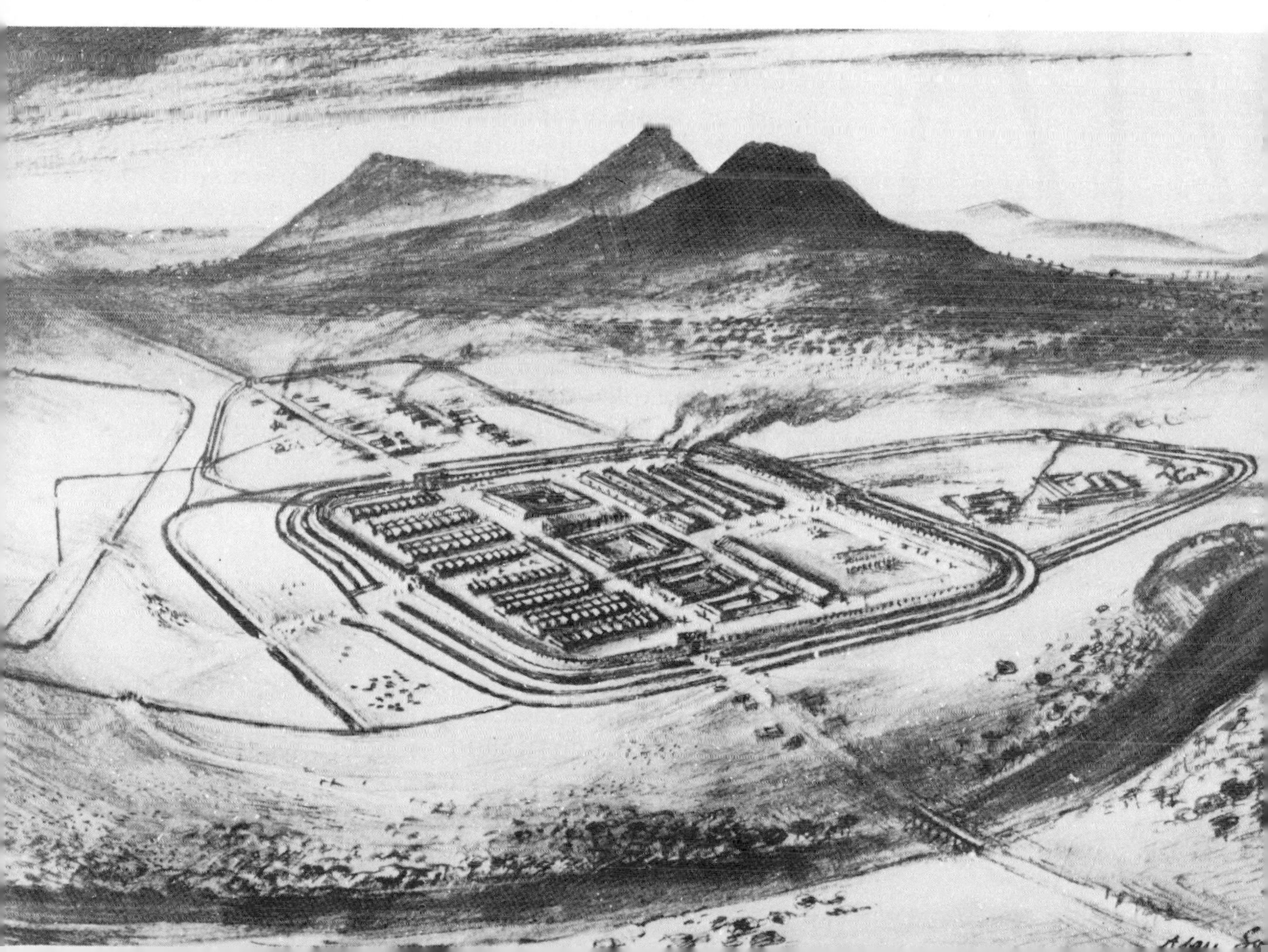

(Top) Roman tools found at Newstead: wooden rake with iron prongs and smiths' tongs
(Bottom) Roman leather boot left behind at Newstead

the floors and through hollows in the walls. Between them and the headquarters stood the granaries, with their floors raised above ground level to keep the grain dry. To the east were the barracks of the legionaries, the Roman *infantry* or foot soldiers. The legionaries were Roman citizens. As citizens they could marry or hold property or become officials helping to control the Empire. To the west were the buildings housing the horses and men of the auxiliary cavalry. These auxiliaries, like the men who defended the walls, were not yet Roman citizens.

Work and Weapons

The size and strength of the Roman walls and forts tell us that the Roman soldier spent far more of his time in building than he ever did in fighting. He had to be prepared to do anything, to build a wall or a barracks, to dig a drain, make roads, store grain or cook the meals. In addition, tools such as hoes, rakes, sickles and scythes, which they left behind at Newstead, tell us that soldiers, or perhaps native people, cleared the forest, cultivated the soil and grew crops. Some soldiers had special jobs: some worked with leather, making and repairing jerkins, harness, boots and shoes; some made armour from fine brass scales, laced together with leather and wire; some made weapons; and some were carpenters. Though all these occupations took up much time, the men were soldiers first and foremost, and would practise fighting for the days when they might march against the Celts or take their turn in guarding the Antonine Wall.

Remains found at Newstead give us a good picture of the Roman soldier. He wore an iron helmet, coming low at the back to protect his neck like a German 'tin hat', and tying under his chin. His jerkin was of leather, and was covered with iron breastplates curved to the shape of his body, or else with scale armour. The legionary wore breeches which reached half-way down the calf of his leg, and over them he had a skirt which looked like a kilt. His boots were heavy with five or six layers of leather on the soles which had tackets in them.

The legionary carried a short stabbing sword with a blade fifty centimetres long, while the auxiliary had a longer slashing sword. Auxiliaries' shields were normally oval, of wood covered with leather and bound with bronze. A short bow was used by the auxiliaries to fire arrows, which, for the first time in this country, had iron heads with three barbs. Spears, too, were carried. Often they were quite short ones

for throwing, but sometimes they were four metres long.

The bath, on the right of the drawing on page 29, was for the legionaries only. Here they took a warm bath, moved on to a sweating room which was filled with hot air, and then into a hot bath. Finally they had a cold plunge to cool off. They did exercises afterwards, and were massaged by attendants who rubbed ointments into their skin. Here, too, they played games. Gaming pieces, such as draughts and dice, have been found, and one soldier left a brooch behind.

Romans and Natives

The Romans held Newstead for two periods, the first lasting until the Celts attacked some time after AD 100. Seeing the invaders sweeping into the fort in force, the Romans, outnumbered and with their forces dispersed, prepared to withdraw. They had to think in a hurry what to do with their valuable equipment.

'Hide it in the wells, quickly! And in the pits! Dump everything, these bowls, that helmet, these querns! Your tools, blacksmith! Cover them up, quickly! Quickly! They're on us!' Broken swords and a split skull bear witness to the struggle. The loss of Newstead was part of a greater disaster and probably the time when the ill-fated Ninth Legion was wiped out.

When the Romans returned, about AD 140, they rebuilt the fort, but did not find the treasures their old comrades had hidden. Roman troops were stationed there during the next sixty years, longer probably than the lifetime of the average man in the second century AD. The men who in recent years dug up Newstead fort found an altar, jugs, beads and coins among the skeletons of unburied animals and men. The Romans had again suddenly been forced to seek shelter on the south side of Hadrian's Wall.

Roman armour and weapons: brass scales from body armour, sword and spearhead

Their stay in the south of Scotland did not, as it did in southern Britain, result in the spread of Roman civilisation. It was a military conquest, achieved by force and maintained by force. Their last attempt to conquer Scotland failed, and the land fell back into the hands of the Celts, although the Romans controlled the south of Britain for two more centuries. Only their roads lasted and were used by traders for hundreds of years afterwards. Even today, the roads from Carlisle to Glasgow, and from Jedburgh to Dalkeith, follow the routes chosen by the Romans for many kilometres.

Something for You to Do

1. A football pitch has an area of about 0.6 hectares. Newstead fort covered six hectares. How many football pitches could have been contained within its walls?
2. *a*) What shape was a Roman fort?
   b) Where was the headquarters and why?
   c) How many gates can you see?
3. Study the picture on page 28. The man on the horse is a Roman cavalryman and the others are Celts. Describe carefully what you see and what you think is happening.
4. *a*) Make two columns under the headings *Legionary* and *Auxiliary* and point out as many differences between them as you can.
   b) Imagine that you are a soldier in Newstead and describe a day in your life.
5. Draw a Roman soldier with his weapons.
6. An exciting book on the Romans in Scotland is *Word to Caesar* by Geoffrey Trease.

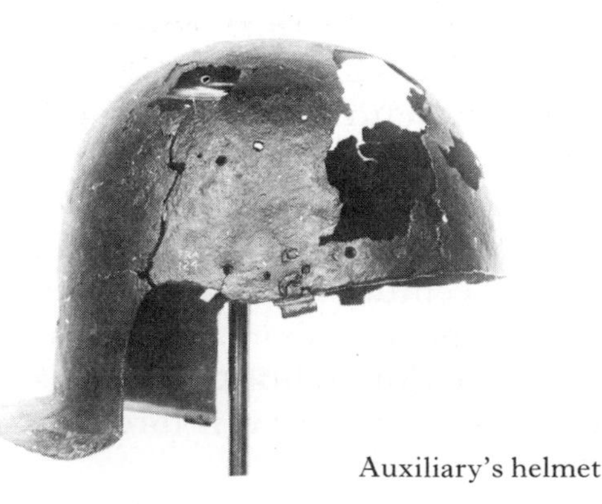

Auxiliary's helmet

7 The Making of Scotland

A period of four hundred years, as long as all the time since John Knox and Mary Queen of Scots, is a remarkable time for any empire to last, especially when it is ruled from a single city. Neither Rome nor even the whole of Italy could find enough young men to defend it. More and more of the conquered peoples were joining the Roman armies, until not even the generals were of Roman birth. The Roman Empire had become too big, its thousands of civil servants too great a burden. Great men struggled for power and the poor to keep their families and pay their taxes. The Empire did not collapse because of a revolution inside its borders, but because it could not fight off a new threat from outside.

The Barbarians

It is difficult at first glance to see how Britain could be affected by things happening in eastern Asia. At that time, however, the grasslands there began to dry up, and this set the people, the Huns, on the move. Prevented from going east by the Great Wall of China which had been built to keep them out, these fierce, yellow-skinned and black-haired men turned their shaggy ponies towards the setting sun and swept all before them. The movement of the peoples was on! Fearless horsemen, firing bone-tipped arrows as they rode, they crossed the Urals and the Steppes of Russia. Unable to stand against these cruel conquerors, some of the Germanic tribes, called Goths, asked to be allowed to settle inside the Roman Empire. Later waves of Goths were to form the new kingdoms in the west, the West Goths in Spain, the East Goths in Italy, the Franks in France.

The Romans tried to face the new danger by giving up their more distant lands like Britain and bringing their forces nearer home. But the capital was captured by Alaric the Goth in AD 410, and the greatness of Rome was at an end.

The Making of England

Britain was now open to attack. The peoples of the lower Rhine valley (the Angles, Saxons and Jutes) were caught up in this movement westwards.

Leaving their villages, the separate tribes of Angles, Saxons and Jutes gathered their weapons and rowed across the North Sea in open boats. They were keen seamen who looked on a shipwreck as a good way of gaining experience.

They swarmed round the river mouths, going as far inland as possible before landing. If you look at an atlas, you will notice that most rivers in Britain flow towards the east, making invasion from Europe easier. The invaders fought the Britons on landing, driving them slowly westwards into the highlands of Cornwall, Devon, Wales and the Lake District. They looted and destroyed the Roman forts and towns. Not used to town life, the Anglo-Saxons settled on the banks of rivers or cleared the forests and built villages and cultivated fields as they had done in Germany. They were ruled by small kings but gradually the number of their kingdoms was reduced to three, *Northumbria* (north of the Humber), *Mercia* (in the Midlands) and *Wessex* (occupied by the West Saxons), and by the tenth century they were united into *Angle-land* or 'England'. The newcomers brought their own language, English.

In Wales today many people still speak their own language,

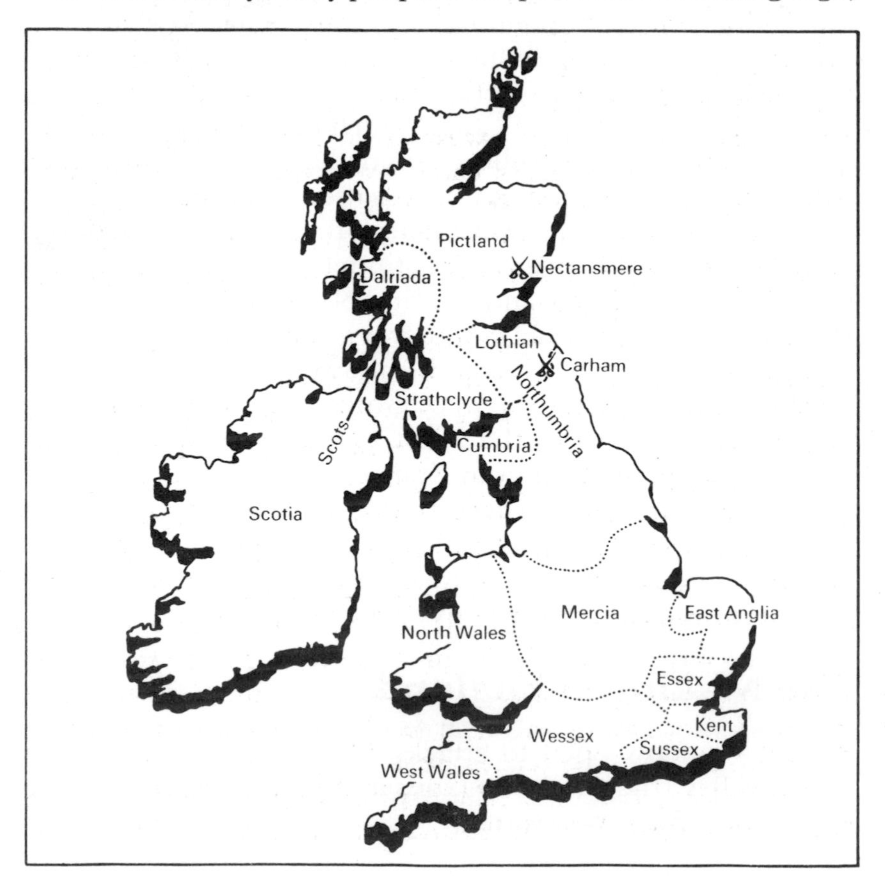

Early kingdoms in Scotland and England

Welsh, which is derived from the common speech of the ancient Britons. It may surprise you to learn that the same language used to be spoken in Scotland also, by the Britons of Strathclyde.

Four Peoples in Scotland

The movement of the peoples affected Scotland too. North of the Forth the people were called the Picts or 'painted men' by the Romans, from their habit of painting their bodies. We do not understand their language, but we do know that they were fierce warriors, who often attacked the Romans in the south. They have left ample proof that they had artists among them because they carved figures of animals, horsemen and foot soldiers on flat slabs. The Picts covered by far the largest area of the country, but much of it was mountainous and the people were widely scattered. In the south-west were the Britons of *Strathclyde* whose capital was on Dumbarton Rock.

Pictish riders, including a woman sitting side-saddle, going hunting with their hounds

So far, we have used the word 'Scotland' to describe the country, but we have said nothing about the Scots. We have, in fact, been describing Scotland before the Scots. Two new peoples arrived: the Angles from the east, sailing up the Forth and Tweed, and the Scots from the west. The Angles drove the native Britons westwards into Galloway and the Clyde valley. The Scots came over in skin-covered boats from Ireland to settle in *Dalriada* in Argyll. This small kingdom of Gaelic-speaking Scots, though cut off from the rest of the country by mountains, was, in time, to give its name to the whole people.

Let us consider how these four peoples were united. There can be no doubt that the spread of the Gospel by the followers of Ninian and Columba gave them all something they shared which was stronger than the mountains or the different languages which divided them. But it was not certain then that Scotland as we know it would ever become an independent kingdom. The Angles of Northumbria controlled most of the land from the Humber to the Forth, and swept northwards into Pictland. In AD 685, however, 'God favoured Brude mac Bile'. This Pictish king and his warriors overwhelmed the Angles at *Nectansmere* near Forfar. This great victory made sure that the land, north of the Tay at least, would remain independent.

In AD 843, Kenneth MacAlpin, King of Scots, became king of the Picts as well. He seems to have had a claim to the

Pictish throne through his mother, at a time when more Scots were coming over from Ireland while the Picts were suffering from Viking raids. This explains why the Scots triumphed and the country became 'Scotland' and not 'Pictland'.

The people between the Forth and the Cheviots became part of the northern kingdom by the middle of the eleventh century. The Angles of Lothian in the east were certainly under the rule of King Malcolm II of Scotland by 1018, after his victory over the English at *Carham-on-Tweed.* Sixteen years later, Malcolm was succeeded as king by his grandson, Duncan, king of the Britons of Strathclyde. Duncan I was the first king to rule over the whole of Scotland, as we know it, except for the north and west which were in the grip of the Vikings (see chapter 9).

Something for You to Do

1. *a*) Name three kingdoms formed by the Goths in Europe.
   b) Name the early kingdoms formed by Anglo-Saxons in England.
   c) Draw a map to show the four peoples who made up Scotland.
2. *a*) Which people occupied your part of the country?
   b) Try to find traces of them. The names of places near you will help, if you find some like those in the chart below.

Name	Language	Meaning	Place
Pit	Pictish	Bit of farmland or farm steading	*Pittodrie* (croft by the wood, or, on the slope) *Pitlochry* (stony piece of land)
Bal	Gaelic	Village	*Ballindalloch* (village in the field) *Ballachulish* (village on the straits)
Kil	Gaelic	Church	*Kilbride* (church of St Brigid)
Caer	British	Fort	*Caerlaverock* (fort of the lark)
Pen	British	Hill	*Penpont* (hill by the bridge)
Ton	English	Village	*Swinton* (Swein's toun)
Ham	English	Home or Village	*Tyninghame* (village of the people by the River Tyne)

3. Make a time chart, covering the years from AD 400 to 1100, and insert the main events from this chapter. Keep adding to it as you read on.

8 The Coming of Christianity

He died that we might be forgiven,
He died to make us good.

You have probably met or listened to a missionary home from India or Africa, and heard him describe how he lived among the natives, teaching the children, healing the sick and telling them about the life and the example of Jesus Christ and his death on the cross. In the early centuries after the birth of Christ, our ancestors had not heard the Gospel, the 'good news'. *They* were the heathen peoples, and to them the missionaries came.

We know little about the religion of our ancestors in early times. The people were mystified by the world around them, and worshipped what they welcomed but did not understand. Led by the Druids, they worshipped the rising sun, the giver of light and warmth. Some of the things people do today at Beltane feasts and Hallowe'en have come down from early religions.

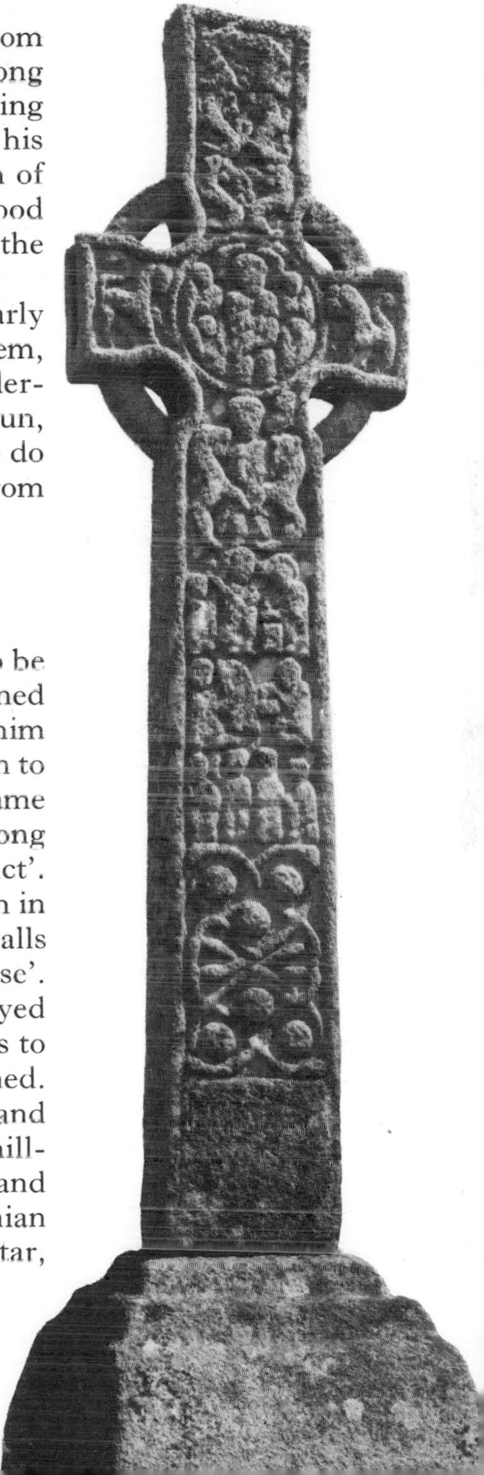

St Ninian

Ninian grew up among the Britons, and went to Rome to be educated. There he was eventually made a bishop, and joined the great St Martin at Tours in France. St Martin taught him to go away on his own at times to think and pray, and then to return to the world to spread the word of God. He became our first known missionary, when he returned to live among the Britons, in the 'no man's land between Roman and Pict'. In AD 397, he and his helpers built the first known church in Scotland, at *Whithorn* in Galloway. They covered its walls with white plaster, and it was known as the 'white house'. This was the headquarters of the mission, where they prayed and worked and ate together. Local chiefs sent their sons to school there and young missionaries came to be trained. Dressed in cloaks of undyed wool and carrying book and staff, the missionaries set out to preach to the folk in the hill-top forts. They converted the people of the south-west, and worked their way north. Churches dedicated to St Ninian were built at Glasgow, Eccles near Stirling, Dunottar, Methlick in Aberdeenshire, and Navidale in Sutherland.

St Martin's Cross, Iona

Many places have a connection with a local saint. Glasgow, for example, claims St Kentigern (Mungo), Culross in Fife has St Serf, whose retreat ('desert') was, tradition tells us, at Dysart. Try to find out who was the missionary in your district. Often the oldest church, the parish church, is dedicated to St Mary, but the names of other churches sometimes provide clues to local saints.

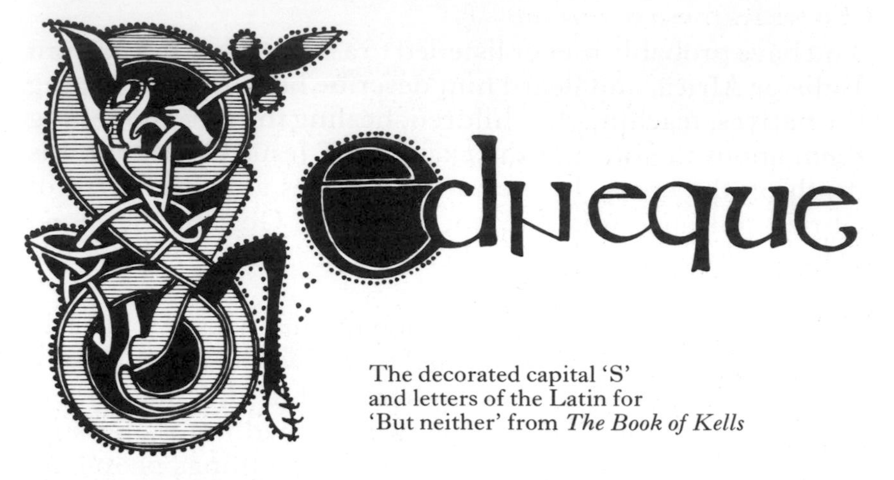

The decorated capital 'S' and letters of the Latin for 'But neither' from *The Book of Kells*

St Columba

The Scots, you will remember, came from Ireland. It was also from Christian Ireland that Columba came, not as a young man dedicated to the Church, but as a high-born prince disgraced in his own country. A quarrel over who owned a copy of the Psalms which he was making led to a battle which drove him to exile himself. In AD 563, he set out to find a place from which he would not be able to see the shores of Ireland again.

He and his twelve companions pushed off in their boats in the same direction as their fellow-Scots had gone, towards Dalriada. Tossed like corks on the Atlantic waves, they came at last to the windswept island of *Iona*, off the west coast of Mull. Here was a place of loneliness and silence, yet near enough to the Scots of Dalriada, and here they built their church. They were a simple, self-supporting community, living in separate huts round the church, with only such other buildings as were necessary. There was the kitchen, the guest-house (for they made a 'fuss' of strangers), the stable, the workshop and the granary. They kept flocks, ploughed the land and fished. Like the followers of St Ninian they lived humbly, having nothing to call their own. Columba himself, we are told, had only a stone for a pillow.

They loved learning. After all, Columba had left Ireland because of the secret copy he had made of the Psalms. Lovingly they copied the sacred words of the Gospels. An example of their work, which was begun in Iona, is the beautiful *Book of Kells*, now in Trinity College, Dublin. The standard of decoration was very high, as you can see from the illustration, and writing was tiring and difficult, as the monk who wrote these words tells us:

> My hand is weary with writing
> My sharp quill is not steady
> My slender-beaked pen pours forth
> A black draught of shining dark-blue ink.

They paddled their little boats to northern islands like Skye. They went up the long sea lochs, and travelled across Perthshire and Fife, bringing to the Picts the story of Christ. Columba himself, fearless of robber and wolf, reached Inverness, where he may have converted King Brude as well as some of the Picts.

For years Columba and his disciples made Iona the religious centre of the north. He was a strong, rugged, commanding figure, but at the same time a kind, friendly man, who loved children and animals. When he was very old, and knew that he was going to die, he climbed the slope above the church and blessed the island with these words:

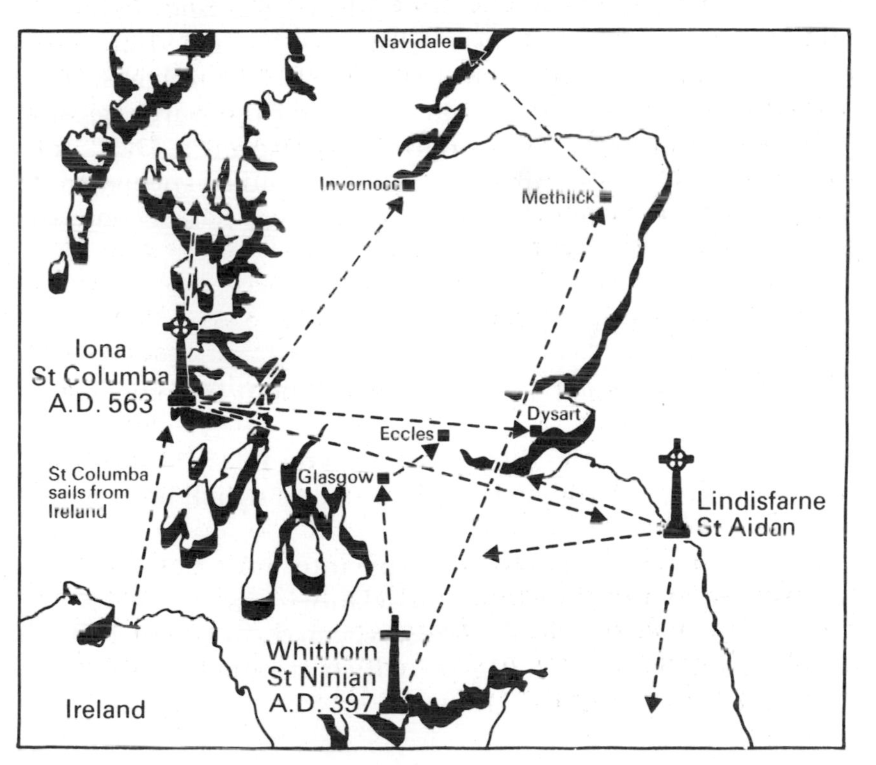

The spread of Christianity in Scotland

> Unto this place, small and mean though it be, great homage shall yet be paid, not only by the kings and peoples of the Scots, but by the rulers of barbarous and distant nations with their people. Thy saints also, of other churches, shall regard it with no common reverence.

So indeed they have, and with reason. Christianity, being shared by the Picts and the Scots, helped them to join together as one nation. St Aidan left Iona and made *Lindisfarne* (Holy Island) his home for his work in converting Northumbria (which included what is now south-east Scotland). To carry on Aidan's work, St Cuthbert left his sheep on the Lammermuir hills to tend a human flock.

Most of England, however, received the Gospel from St Augustine and his followers, who had come from Rome. Roman Christianity in southern England and eventually (by the decision taken at the *Synod of Whitby* in AD 664) in Northumbria as well, helped to unify the English, and to separate them from the northern peoples, the children of Whithorn and Iona.

St Andrew with his cross

St Andrew

'Why', you may ask, 'is St Andrew the patron saint of Scotland?' This is the reason. Andrew, the first of Jesus's disciples, was crucified on a saltire, or X-shaped cross, in Greece. Some of his bones were carried to a church in what is now the town of St Andrews in Fife, and this church became the most important in Scotland. St Andrew's Day, 30th November, is remembered as Scotland's special day, particularly by Scots abroad, and his cross has become the national flag.

Something for You to Do

1. Make a drawing of Columba's settlement in Iona, as you imagine it looked.
2. Who converted the district where you live? Think about any churches, halls, stations and streets which have saints' names.
3. Under the heading 'Iona', copy into your notebook the blessing of St Columba on the island.
4. Look at the shape of St Andrew's cross in the picture on this page. Draw the flag on which it appears (white on a blue background).

9 The Vikings

It is high tide on Iona, on a summer morning in the year 806.

The shepherd looks out to sea, attracted by the screeching of sea birds. There's a boat with a sail, another and another, eight in all, riding proudly on the waves. He peers into the distance in fear. Can it be . . . ? He sees the raven on the sail of the foremost ship. The Vikings are coming, the demons, the plunderers, the killers. He runs through the heather, down the slope to the church.

'They're coming, they're coming!' he screams. The brothers understand at once. There have been raids before.

The bell tolls. The abbot tries to comfort the monks and leads them in prayer. He orders the ornaments and precious writings to be hidden, and walks out to meet the invaders. They are landing now from their long, narrow boats, which they have drawn up high on the sand. Look at them—tall men, fierce men, all with round shields, terrifying battle-axes and swords. The abbot stands before them, pleading with them to leave his church in peace. They brush him aside, and rush to the settlement. Some make for the byre, drive the cows down to the shore, and kill them there for food. Most of them hurry into the church. They catch the monks storing

their treasures under stone slabs. Axes swing, swords flash and monks fall dead. With straw and a light the church is set on fire. The brethren outside kneel and pray, but are put to the sword. Sixty-eight people on the island become martyrs, and the Vikings go back to their ships, laden with treasures and supplies.

Let us see who these invaders were, and how and why they came.

The Vikings as Sailors

They were great sea warriors, who came from Scandinavia. If you look at a map of this land, made up of Norway, Sweden and Denmark, you will see that much of it is mountainous, and that the west coast is cut into by a great many *fiords*. In the time of the Vikings the hill-land was poor, so that the men looked to the sea for a living. Having discovered how to make iron, they made tools to cut down trees, and used the wood to make boats. They fished, but soon the sea beckoned them further, and they became explorers and raiders.

Their boats were long and wide but could be sailed in shallow water and also be hauled up on a beach on a summer raid. Often decorated with the head and tail of a dragon, they were driven by oars and one large sail. They were easy to steer by their side rudder on long sea voyages.

On their early expeditions, the Vikings sailed to plunder other lands. Naturally, the best places to raid, in their eyes, contained not only food, drink and clothing, but also gold and silver ornaments to take back to their womenfolk.

The St Ninian's Isle treasure, twenty-eight silver bowls and brooches, was discovered by a boy under the floor of a little church in Shetland in 1958. It probably belonged to a chief who had it stored there for safety. This may be another reason why holy places suffered so many attacks, and why the monks feared the Vikings and welcomed the bad weather, as an Irish monk tells us in the margin of his manuscript:

> The bitter wind is high to-night;
> It lifts the white locks of the sea.
> In such wild winter storm no fright
> Of savage Viking troubles me.

The Vikings returned home to spend the winter building boats, making weapons, eating, drinking and telling stories in their halls high above the fiords. Their love of adventure and their feeling for the sea made them great sailors and

Viking weapons

explorers. They knew nothing of the compass, although they sailed in their great ships to new lands – Shetland, Orkney, the Faroes, Iceland and Greenland. Usually they sailed westwards, reaching out towards the setting sun. They found their way by using rough-and-ready rules. Sailing to Greenland, for example, they passed the Faroes at a distance from which the sea appeared halfway up the mountains. They sailed south of Iceland at a distance from which wild-fowl and whales could be seen, and westwards to a point in Greenland just north of Cape Farewell. Try to follow this voyage of the Vikings on a map.

The Vikings as Settlers

Erik the Red discovered Greenland and settled there. His son, Leif Erikson, was the first man to sail direct from Greenland to Norway and back. Later, about AD 1000, Leif sailed along the coast of North America, which he called

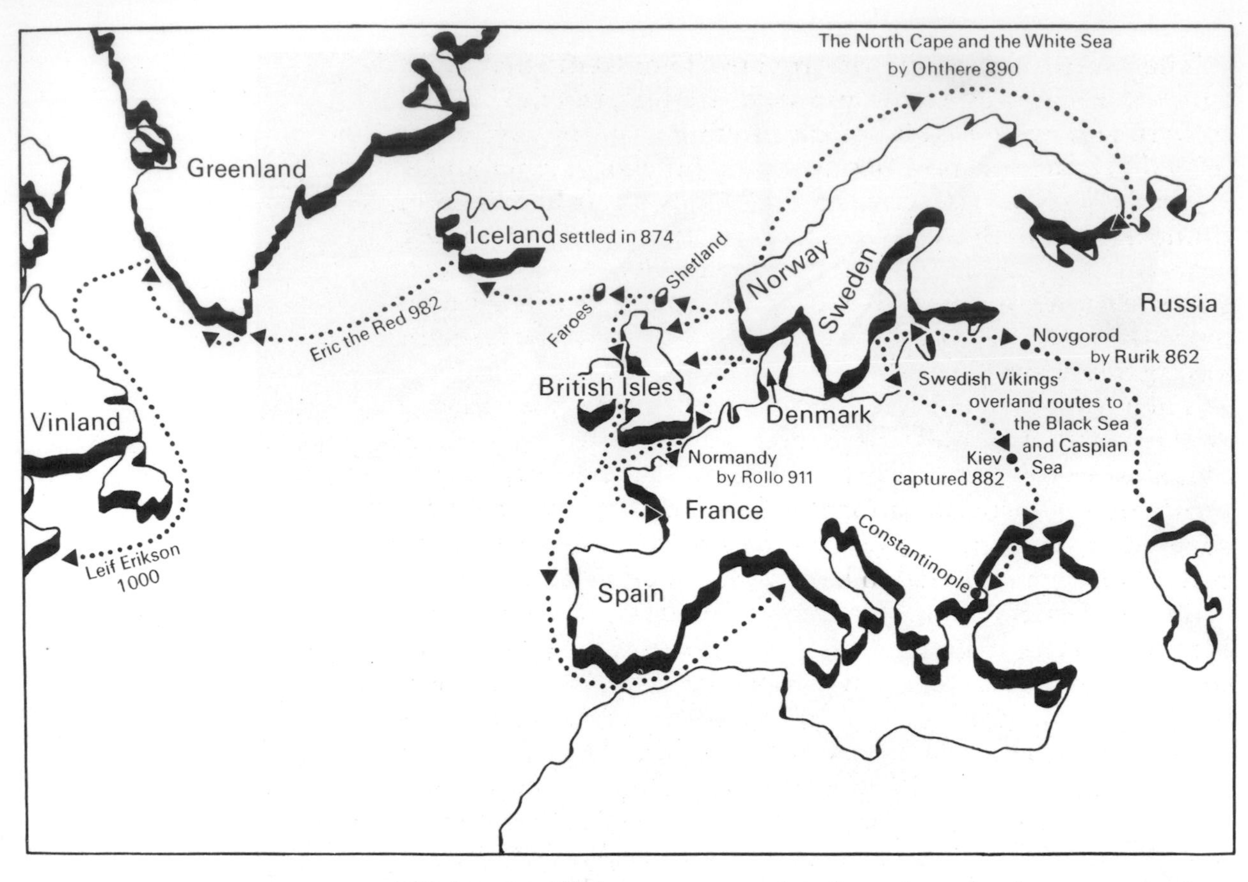

The Vikings as explorers

Vinland. This was nearly five hundred years before Columbus 'discovered' America.

For centuries the Vikings searched for lands which were like their own but better, where they could live in the same way but make a living with less effort. They became land-winners or settlers. Under the leadership of Rurik, they entered and gave a name to Russia; under Rollo they occupied Normandy, the land of the Northmen in France; under Guthrum and later kings Sweyn and Canute, they settled in England. Shetland, Orkney, Caithness and Sutherland, the Hebrides, Ireland, the Faroes, Iceland and Greenland all became Viking lands, and the North Atlantic almost a Viking lake.

The Viking *Sagas* tell of the hardships they faced and the heroic deeds they performed, while conquering these new lands. They tell us who the foremost Vikings were. Some warriors were given surnames which described their looks: Harold Fairhair, Erik the Red, Helgi the Lean and Onund Woodenleg; some their dress: Ragnar Hairy-breeks and Magnus Bareleg; and some because of their reputation in battle: Erik Bloodaxe and Thorfinn Skullsplitter.

They were not merely destroyers. They kept their links with the sea by pirate raids and slave-trading, but they fished as well, and even used boats for moving crops of hay. They settled in lonely parts of Scotland like Jarlshof in Shetland.

Jarlshof was as attractive to the Vikings as it had been to Stone Age and Bronze Age peoples up to three thousand years earlier. The land was fertile, and there were cod to catch and grey seals to hunt. Besides, Viking ships often called there from Orkney on the way to Norway, only forty-eight sailing hours away.

Their homes were longhouses, each one longer than a cricket pitch. The walls were thick, each like two 'dry-stane dykes' side by side, with earth packed in between them. Driftwood was cut up to form low-ridged roofs which were covered with heather, straw or sometimes peat. Stones tied to straw ropes over the thatch kept it secure in the high winds.

The oldest house at Jarlshof, probably the headman's, contained a large living room, with a fire in the middle, and a smaller room (the kitchen) where food was cooked in an oven by the heat of stones taken out of the fire. The house was smoky, and peat soot covered the rafters. The other houses had people and animals living under the same roof. They were 'clarty but cosy'. The outbuildings included a byre, a barn and a smithy, where a hole worn five centimetres deep in a stone anvil is proof that the smith was always hammering on it, making everything from sickles to fishing hooks. People walked along paths of stone slabs, and in the yard there were stone platforms on which hayricks stood.

Their work changed with the seasons. There was sowing in the spring, followed by lambing, sheep-shearing, hay-making, harvesting barley and slaughtering some of the animals before winter set in. They cut peats and dried them in the sun on the hill across the bay. They enjoyed fishing in summer. The sheep-shearing saw the start of another year's cloth-making. Washing, combing and spinning followed one after another until, during the winter evenings, they were ready to weave on an upright loom by the light of little oil lamps. All the year round there were the cattle, sheep and pigs to herd, and in the winter the cows were kept indoors in byre-stalls. The men killed many calves, lambs and young pigs for food. They caught fish and killed sea-birds to get something different to eat. Usually they ate flesh and fish only, bread being kept for feasts.

These crofter-fishermen at Jarlshof were typical of thousands of Vikings who settled on the islands and the mainland of Scotland and brought with them their knowledge of sea-faring and boat-building. The dialects and names of places in the northern islands show how far they spread. For centuries they were a threat to Scottish kings, but they did bring courage, strength and a spirit of adventure to Scotland. Some of us are descended from them.

Something for You to Do

1. Mark on a map of Scotland the islands and counties where the Vikings settled.
2. Look at an atlas for countries with fiord coasts where the Vikings settled, and make a list of them.
3. Name as many weapons as you can see in the picture on page 43.
4. How many surnames like the Viking ones on page 44 can you find or make up?
5. What do you see people doing in the picture of Jarlshof on this page?
6. Draw a Viking ship.
7. If you are interested in the Vikings, you will find a lot more about them in *The Vikings* by Sydney Wood, in Oliver & Boyd's *Exploring History* series.

Jarlshof, a Viking village (reconstruction by Alan Sorrell)

O Malcolm Canmore and St Margaret

By the time of the reign of Malcolm III (1057–93), Scotland was a united country, covering roughly the same area as today. True, the islands and north mainland were subject to the Vikings, but elsewhere the king's word was law. Though the people recognised Malcolm Canmore[1] as king, it is doubtful if they thought of themselves yet as one nation. Local chiefs still had great power. Not all the people spoke the same language. Pictish was dying out, and Gaelic was becoming the language of the Highlanders. In the south of Scotland, English was spoken in the east and was coming to be used in the west. There were also differences in religion, because not all Scotland had been converted by St Columba.

Malcolm Canmore

With so many races in Scotland, it is not surprising that Malcolm's own background was mixed. Half Celtic, half English, he 'had the Gaelic' and spoke English as well. His father, Duncan, had been killed by Macbeth, but not murdered by him, as Shakespeare's play would have us believe. When Macbeth seized the throne, Malcolm had to flee to England for safety. In the south he learned how England and the other countries in Europe were ruled. There, too, although Malcolm was never able to read or write, he had met and admired men of learning. Finally he returned to Scotland and defeated Macbeth at the battle of *Lumphanan* in Aberdeenshire. He became king of Scotland, and set up his capital at Dunfermline.

The Norman Conquest of England

While Malcolm was king in Scotland, England was successfully invaded from Europe. The Normans, who were descendants of the Vikings, had settled in Normandy in France, where they became Christian and learned to speak French. Training and practice made them skilled fighters on horseback. Led by their duke, William, they came across and defeated the English at the battle of *Hastings* in 1066, and William became king of England. The story of the invasion is

[1] *Canmore* was Malcolm's Gaelic nickname. It meant 'Great Head'.

Scene from the Bayeux Tapestry showing Harold, the figure killed by the horseman's sword, not by an arrow, as once was thought

shown in pictures in a magnificent piece of needlework called the *Bayeux Tapestry,* which was made in England not long afterwards.

Harold, the king of the English, had been killed at Hastings. Edgar, the English heir to the throne, had to flee from the Normans with his family including his sister, Margaret. They came north by sea, and landed on the south coast of Fife, in a bay between Rosyth and North Queensferry, which is now known as St Margaret's Hope. Malcolm made the refugees welcome at Dunfermline, and Margaret became his second wife and queen.

St Margaret

Margaret must have seemed to the Scots a strong-willed woman who had very expensive tastes. She delighted in the 'show' of royalty. When the king travelled she saw that he was always escorted by a strong bodyguard on horseback. She made the royal palace a blaze of coloured fabrics and decked the royal table with gold and silver dishes and goblets. Her demands encouraged trade, especially in luxuries.

It should not be thought that Malcolm had married a queen who dominated him and imposed her own foreign will on Scotland. He was a rough, tough warrior whose army invaded the north of England time and again, often with great cruelty. He and she wanted to make Scotland more modern and more religious, and tried to govern it better. Together they took the best of what they knew of Europe as their model. Certainly she helped him to rule the country, the first woman to take part in governing Scotland.

Had she not married, Margaret would have entered a convent and become a nun. A sincere and very religious woman, she did all she could to help the poor. Her ladies learned that she disapproved of riotous laughter. They copied her gracious manners and followed her example in doing good. Margaret did all she could to help the church in Scotland. She invited the first monks to come to Dunfermline, and they began to build the great abbey there. She also provided houses for pilgrims to stay in on either side of the Forth, and they could cross the river by the Queen's Ferry free of charge on their way to St Andrews.

On hearing the news of Malcolm's death during another attack on the north of England, Margaret died in Edinburgh Castle, where her small chapel still stands. Her tomb beside that of her husband in Dunfermline Abbey also became a place of pilgrimage, for Margaret was remembered as a saint.

Something for You to Do

1. Why do you think it was difficult for Malcolm Canmore to rule Scotland in the eleventh century?
2. Draw a Norman horseman from the Bayeux Tapestry.
3. *a*) What did Margaret do, *i)* for the king, *ii)* for the Church?
   b) Do you know anything called 'St Margaret's' today?

Inside St Margaret's Chapel, Edinburgh Castle

11 David I and Norman Ways

Although William had been crowned king of England, he still needed men to fight against the English until he controlled the whole country. Then he had to reward them. He did this not with money, but with land. Norman lords were given areas of land if they swore to obey the king and bring a fixed number of knights to fight for him when he needed them. In this way, a lord became the king's tenant (from the French word *tenir*, to hold), holding land in return for military service. Lords who held land directly from the king were called *tenants-in-chief*. They did not normally wish to keep a great number of knights in their own houses. So they kept a large piece of land for themselves, and gave the rest to their tenants. These men swore an *oath of homage*, to become 'the lord's man' and promised to bring a smaller number of knights for the king. They might divide up their lands, too, keeping part for themselves and splitting the rest between their knights. Holding land like this is called *feudalism*.

There were a number of ways in which the Normans differed from the English. They were foreigners who spoke French. They had gained land and become a new landed aristocracy. They were *over* the English. Roughly speaking, they were the lords and knights, and the English became serfs and had to work for them. They were knights, trained to fight on horseback. For protection they wore a hauberk, a long leather coat covered by metal rings, with slits at the back and front to allow them to sit comfortably on their horses. Their helmets were cone-shaped, with a strip of metal coming down in front to protect the nose. The lance was their chief weapon but they carried swords as well. They occupied castles at important places, to keep the English down. They even looked different, with their shaved chins and their hair cut short at the back and sides.

David, Earl of Huntingdon

To avoid the trouble in Scotland after the deaths of Malcolm and Margaret, their younger children were sent to England to be brought up. David went to the court of William Rufus, where he became a scholar and a knight. This is important in our history because David brought many of the latest European ideas from England.

David was Earl of Huntingdon in England, and had other lands as well. He was one of the chief nobles at the court and a trusted adviser of the next English king, Henry I. David saw from the inside how a good king ruled and learned much.

Arms of Robert the Bruce's family as earls of Carrick in Ayrshire

David and the Normans

The Normans came to England as invaders and stayed on because they had conquered it. Scotland suffered no Norman conquest. The Normans came north because David invited them. When he became King of Scots, he brought some of his Norman friends with him. Many of their names are common names in Scotland today, names like Bruce, Lindsay, Montgomery, Graham and Somerville. Normans who followed later included Melvilles, Fairbairns, Archibalds and Ramsays.

Feudalism in Scotland

In parts of Scotland, as in England, feudalism was introduced. The newcomers were given land, on condition that they brought knights to fight for David. For example, an early Robert de Brus (Bruce) was given Annandale in return for the service of ten knights. He swore an oath of homage to the king, promising 'to be his man' and another of *fealty*, like this:

> I, Robert, swear on these holy Gospels of God that henceforth I shall be faithful to you, as a vassal ought to be to his lord. You will never lose life or limb, nor the honour you have, by my will, advice, or encouragement, but in all those things I shall be your helper according to my power.

Arms of the Ramsays who came to Scotland not long after David I died

This suited the king. In return for the land they held, the lords all promised to obey him. Notice that they did not own the land, for it was all the king's: they 'held' it. Even today, by the law of 'treasure trove' in Scotland, anything found on or in the ground belongs to the Crown. 'What belongs to no one belongs to the king.' Each lord kept his own men in order. From the king's point of view, it helped him to rule the country, and it gave him horsemen for his army without having to pay them.

The king would go to the lands he granted and pace out or ride the limits, pointing out boundary marks like 'the old oak tree', or 'the big round stone', since there were no maps. Details of the land he was giving and the services the tenant was to give were written down on a *charter*, which was signed and sealed before witnesses. This was the lord's legal title to his land. It was also the first sign that the king was having letters written by his civil service. These men were all churchmen, because they were the only people who could write.

Churches and Castles

The land of a lord or tenant became known as his *domain*. Near its centre was his tower or fortified house. The church was built close by and it served the *parish* which was usually the same size as the lord's domain. The priest had the lord to protect him and collected the *tithes*, the tenth of every man's produce from the land which was due to the Church to keep the priest and the poor. The finest existing Norman parish church in Scotland is at Dalmeny, near Edinburgh. Notice in the picture the rounded arches over its door and windows.

The king built castles in many places. Wherever there was a royal castle David would place a Norman baron to be his sheriff, to maintain law and order in the surrounding countryside. This area became a *shire*, with the castle, and later the town which grew up beside it, as its centre or capital. The sheriff was also in charge of defending it and collecting

Dalmeny Church with its round Norman arches. The square tower is modern, but it looks just like a Norman one

taxes, although the main duty of a sheriff today is to deal with serious offences brought before his court.

Sheriffs, and indeed all tenants-in-chief, could expect that the king and his court would come to see them from time to time. The government was not fixed in one place. It moved about with the king on his travels throughout the land. In this way the king found out for himself what was going on in all parts of his kingdom. Besides, he could keep himself and his court by living for three or four days on the feasts each lord they visited was expected to provide.

Burghs, Abbeys and Trade

The royal castles were signs that the king was strong. The abbeys, founded by the monks whom David had invited from England and France, showed that he was trying to make Scotland more religious and more civilised. When he made certain villages into royal burghs, he took the first important step to encourage industry and trade. The first Scottish coins, silver pennies, were minted at Roxburgh and Berwick during his reign. Previously, foreign coins had been in use. Though the use of money was not yet common, it made trade with foreign countries easier. Measurements, too, were laid down. An inch (2.54 cm) was the length of three good barley grains laid end to end, while an ell, roughly a yard, measured thirty-seven inches (94 cm).

By the changes he introduced David I made Scotland a more advanced country, and gave it a pattern of life which was to last for four hundred years.

Something for You to Do

1. In class, choose a king, one tenant-in-chief, two tenants and four knights. Now act the ceremony of swearing an oath of fealty. Each man swears the oath to the lord immediately above him, and, if that lord is not the king, he should add the words, 'except the faith that I owe to the king'.
2. If anyone in your class has a Norman surname write it down and make a list of other 'Normans' you know.
3. In what ways did Scotland become more modern in the reign of David I?
4. For more about the Normans in England and Scotland, see *Living Under The Normans* in Oliver & Boyd's *Exploring History* series.

12 Life in the Castle

Wooden Castles

The first castles in Scotland were all the king's. When he was deciding where to build a castle, he had to ask himself:

1) *Is there a good water-supply?* (If you visit Edinburgh Castle, look for the two wells.)
2) *Will it be easy to defend?* Usually an outstanding crag or a little hill was a good place, especially at a loop in a river or where two rivers met. Where there were no hills they could make one. They would dig a ditch in a circle and throw all the earth inwards to make a huge mound, called a *motte* (or sometimes *mote*). The ditch, whether it had water in it or not, was called a *moat*. At Inverurie in the north-east, Hawick in the Borders and Mote of Urr in Galloway mottes can still be seen, on which men once built the kind of towers described in the lines below:

> Upon a great dark-coloured rock
> He had his house right nobly set
> Built all about with wattle-work
> Upon the summit was a tower
> That was not made of stone and lime.

None of these wooden castles has lasted but the stone castle at Duffus near Elgin is built on the same plan. If you were a friend visiting this kind of castle, you would cross the water in the moat by the bridge. A sentry opens the strong

What a motte and bailey castle looked like

gate, the only way in. All round the castle is a wall of earth with a *palisade*, a fence of pointed sticks, on top. You are now in a flat, grassy area, called the *bailey*. Close to the track you see the byres and stables and pens where all the beasts will be driven tonight for safety. On the left you see servants carrying a side of beef to the kitchen next to the hall. You will eat and be entertained with everyone else tonight, by the big fire in the hall.

You dismount, a man leads your horse away to the stable, while you cross to the motte and clamber up the steps to the tower. You pause and look up. The tower is plain and solid, built of hefty timbers. In times of danger the lord and his family sleep in this tower. The sentry on top has been watching you. He recognises you and waves his hand. You are in a *motte and bailey castle*.

David I's Norman barons built themselves castles like these. They were places where people felt safer but there was not much room in a wooden tower, and it was always in danger of being burned down.

A castle entrance. The portcullis is the iron grating here raised to allow people to enter

Stone Castles

In the late twelfth century kings, then barons, began to build stone castles. These were stronger and had more room inside. They could be of many different shapes. You can still see some of these castles today. Caerlaverock in Dumfriesshire, for example, was built in the shape of a triangle on an island in a marsh. It has great round towers at two corners and a strong gateway with a tower on each side of it. Inverlochy Castle in Inverness-shire is square with a round tower at each corner, whereas Rothesay Castle is round and its towers, too, are round.

Defence

Stone castles had thick walls, sometimes nearly three metres in width. The two main buildings were the tower and the hall. As the weakest part of the castle was the doorway, the occupants did everything they could to strengthen it. A *drawbridge* might be raised up to prevent enemies from reaching it. An iron grill called a *portcullis*, dropped down in front of the iron-studded door, would protect it. The top of the tower was reached by a dark spiral staircase, rising and turning clockwise. This took away from a right-handed attacker the freedom to slash with his sword. The sentry on

the platform walk on top of the battlements would always be on the lookout for friend or stranger moving towards the stronghold.

As time passed, some castles were built with thicker walls to try to stand against attacks with cannon, but some barons wanted to have strong castles just to make others think they were great men. Even the smaller landowners, the lairds, built towers as fortified places to live in like Smailholm Tower on page 109. These towers, or their ruins, can be seen in many places in Scotland today. They are usually built in the shape of a rectangle, but some have a wing attached, making an L-shape to provide more rooms and more comfort.

The Hall

The hall became the centre of castle life as kings and barons liked to be more comfortable. We know, for instance, that James II did not 'rough it' in Edinburgh Castle. He had a feather mattress and a pillow, and enjoyed wine and salmon. The king's room at Stirling had glass windows. The palace at Falkland had a park and beautiful gardens. He could play tennis, for example, or have a game of cards or chess, or play his guitar. What he did the barons copied.

Even so, it is doubtful whether we should have considered a castle comfortable. Gay tapestries covered some of the stone walls and a rug lay by the fireplace, but most rooms were entered through arches with no doors, and the wind whistled through the long, narrow window-slits, which had to be stuffed with rags in winter. The castle was draughty and dark. At night, fir splinters or lamps burning fish or animal oil gave some light, but they made the rooms smoky and smelly. Floors covered in rushes became refuse heaps when scraps fell from the tables. Dogs wandered about. The place smelled of food and filth, and animals and people. Although men and women washed their hands at the table, they seldom washed their whole bodies. One writer, in fact, described the Middle Ages in Europe as 'a thousand years without a bath'. All the rubbish and slops from the castle were tossed into the moat. Better not to be thrown in there yourself!

In big castles the hall was the place where the king or lord ate in company and in public. He, his family and his guests, sat at a raised table, and were served by squires. The 'salt-fat' or salt container stood in the centre of the table, and poorer people had to sit 'below the salt' or else at separate tables. The food was placed on the table, and the important people helped themselves first. Dishes were of silver or wood, and a dagger was handy for cutting meat. For eating, people used spoons and their fingers, as forks had not yet been invented. When the meal was over, people stayed in the hall and drank. They told stories, listened to the minstrel or laughed at the jester. The ladies might go off to spin and weave, make tapestries [woven pictures] or sew napkins and cloths.

The People in Castles

The men in the castle had to defend it and keep up its supply of food. Many animals were killed in November, then cured and hung in the cellars, while the granaries were kept full of grain. Pepper and other expensive spices bought from merchants made their food more tasty. The king and the barons enjoyed hunting for deer and wild boar in great areas of wasteland called *forest*, such as Ettrick Forest near Selkirk. This was a good way of getting fresh meat.

Attached to the larger royal castles, you would meet men with many different jobs: *bailies* who collected taxes, *fletchers* who made arrows, *lorimers* who made spurs and stirrups, *porters* (door-keepers), as well tailors and cooks, foresters and falconers. Many of them worked in the outbuildings on the bailey. John the cook and William the falconer in time were called John Cook and William Falconer, and this is how many common surnames started.

Something for You to Do

1. Make a drawing of a motte and bailey castle.
2. Go and see the castle nearest to your home. Look for features in it you have read about here. Try to find out:
   a) Who built it
   b) Why it was built there
   c) Where the stone came from.
3. Make a list of these terms and their meanings: *motte, palisade, bailey, hall, drawbridge, portcullis, moat, fletcher, lorimer*.
4. Either *a*) write an eye-witness account of 'How we defended the castle against an enemy attack', or *b*) write about 'My day in the castle'.
5. To tell the difference between a motte and a moat remember 'You could sail a b-o-a-t- on a m-o-a-t'.

13 From Serf to Freeman

In modern times, we think of the 'country' as being away from the towns and cities where most of the people now live. We talk of going out 'into the country', among planted woods and scattered farms. But in Norman times nearly everybody lived in the country, not on farms standing on their own, but in hamlets or little groups of houses called *touns*. 'Ton' at the end of the name of a place, such as Haddington, means a 'toun' or village.

There were a few towns, not of great importance at first, and these were called *burghs*. They were really touns which kings or barons or the Church had made into more important places.

Serfs

When David I granted land to barons or the abbeys, he gave them the touns and the people in them too. Every piece of land had its lord, and in David I's reign a law said that if there was any man 'that hes no propir lord', he must find one within fifteen days or be fined eight cows, a huge sum. Every toun became subject to a lord or an abbot and the men had to perform certain duties for him in return for their lands. Some of them were free but most were serfs. Some were sold, as Turkil Hog and his sons and daughters were to the Prior of Coldingham for three merks of silver (£2). Halden and his brother William and their family, on the other hand, were given by the Earl of Dunbar to the Abbey of Kelso. Serfs belonged to their masters, and might have iron collars to show what they were and whose men they were. They could not leave the toun or change their jobs. This shows they were not free, but they did have some land, and in those unruly days it was often safer to have a lord's protection.

Farming

The lands of the toun were worked as a whole, the men helping one another in the fields. They farmed to feed themselves and clothe themselves. This is called *subsistence farming*.

Ploughing a rig

Not all the land was cultivated. Marshy places along the river were too wet to grow anything. The rest of the land was divided into two parts: the patches of *infield*, nearer to the toun, which always had crops on them, and the *outfield*, rougher ground further away, which was used mainly for pasture. From time to time, some parts of the outfield were ploughed and planted (but no manure was put on them) until the yield was so low that they were allowed to grow grass again. To grow crops year after year on the same soil, manure is needed, and all the manure from the byres and wood-ash from the cottage fires were carted out to the infield. This land was divided into long strips called *rigs* or ridges which were ploughed up and down the slope to let the water run off. Each villager's rigs were scattered in different parts of the infield to ensure that good and bad land were equally shared. Holding land like this is called *run-rig*.

The heavy wooden plough needed from six to twelve oxen yoked to it to pull it. No villager owned so many but each lent one or two to make up the plough-team. At least three men were needed to handle the plough. One man guided it from behind, another put his weight on it to keep the sock down in the furrow, while the third man kept the oxen moving. Turning them was difficult, because they were yoked together in pairs and not harnessed like horses. This probably explains why the rigs were so long and narrow. As much land as possible could then be ploughed with the least number of turns. Other workers would shift big stones and break up hard clods of earth with wooden mallets. Then they would sow seed broadcast by hand, and there was always weeding to be done.

When harvest-time came, mowers stooped to cut the corn with their sickles. Others bound the stalks into bundles and set them up in stooks to dry. Oats were the main crop, for they made oatmeal and oatcakes, while barley was grown for brewing into beer. Pease and beans, cabbages and kale were the main vegetables; turnips and potatoes had not yet been introduced to Britain.

The cattle and sheep of the village grazed on the common pasture or the outfield with the 'toun-herd' ever on the look-out for wolves. About November, when food for the animals became scarce, the weakest ones were slaughtered. The beef and mutton were salted to provide a stock of food for the family throughout the winter.

In the Highlands and other hill areas it was more difficult to grow crops and most people kept animals. On high land, or where only small patches of ground could be tilled, the spade and the *caschrom* took the place of the plough. The caschrom has been called an early plough, but in using it a man works backwards and turns the soil from right to left, that is, in the opposite way to the plough.

Besides growing crops and keeping animals, the people had many other things to do. There was wood to collect and peat to cut, corn to grind and bread to bake, sheep to shear, yarn to spin and cloth to make (usually the 'hodden grey', undyed wool). These were all jobs in which boys and girls could help.

The old dwelling-house might have to be repaired or rebuilt. It was probably built of stone on a wooden framework like the one on page 61, and roofed with turf or heather. There might be a hole in the roof, not directly over the fire, as a chimney. Inside, all was dark when the door and the window-shutters (used instead of glass) were closed. The cows were often under the same roof.

Furniture was what they made themselves: a table, a bench to sit on, combs, spindles, whorls and a loom for making cloth. The family slept on straw or heather on the earthen floor. Since there was not much cleaning to be done, women spent most of their time making cloth and helping in the fields.

The Coming of Freedom

At Medilham (Midlem) toun,
on the land of the Abbey of Kelso, in 1250.

It is just after sunrise on a September morning, and a husbandman [a man with 10 hectares of land] and his son are milking their cows.

'It will be a fine morning to start the harvest,' says the father. 'We should manage to cut one rig of oats to-day, with your mother and the girls to help. Go and sharpen the sickles when you finish with that cow.'

'Yes, father,' replies Adam, 'It will be a change from weeding. The weeds grow as fast as we can cut them.'

But as he goes out of the byre, he hears a voice, the voice of a man on a shaggy pony, the steward from the Abbey grange.

'Come on, all you men! All of you to the grange to cut the corn for the Abbey.'

'But we are going to cut our own corn,' mutters Adam.

A ruined farm cottage in Caithness. Notice the wooden cruck framework holding up the roof

'Quiet, boy,' his father reproves him. 'We must do as we are told.'

'We shall need you all till the crop is cut,' the steward goes on. 'You husbandmen must do five days' work, and the cottars must come till the work is finished. Come to-day, and every dry day until you have done the service you owe.'

'Reaping and carrying their corn, shearing their sheep, ploughing their land,' thinks Adam, fingering his iron collar. 'I wish we had only our own work to do.'

By 1290, Adam had his wish. Each of the husbandmen of Medilham held his land, in return for a rent of eleven shillings a year. They had a struggle to pay the rent, for eleven shillings was a lot of money in the Middle Ages, but at least they were now free men.

And, by the time the Scots had won their independence at Bannockburn in 1314, many more of the people were free tenants of the land they farmed.

Something for You to Do

1. Find from a map as many touns as you can in your district. The name for settlements on page 58 will help you.
2. Under the heading *Subsistence Farming*, make two columns, the first giving the crops and animals of the toun, and the second saying what each was used for.
3. For the names of the parts of a plough see Book 2, page 23.
4. In what ways was it a) good and b) hard to be a free man?
5. Make a drawing of a toun.
6. Make a model of a peasant's house. Use plasticine for the walls, which should be roughened to look like stone. Tie twigs together in pairs to form the rafters, and stick the ends into the tops of the front and back walls. String between the twigs will hold the roof of hay or foam rubber. String weighted with stones at each end may be laid over the thatch to hold it down.

14 The Rise of the Burghs

'The Royal and Ancient Burgh of...' Many a town in Scotland is proud if it can claim to be royal and more ancient than its neighbours. This reminds us that burghs did not simply grow out of small villages. A burgh was *created* by being given a charter, written and sealed, listing its rights, privileges and duties.

If a burgh gained its charter from the king, it became a *royal burgh*, if from a lord or from the Church a *burgh of barony*. The distinction became important in later times, because only the royal burghs sent representatives to the Convention of Royal Burghs and to Parliament. In David I's reign there were fifteen royal burghs: Aberdeen, Berwick, Dunfermline, Edinburgh, Elgin, Forres, Haddington, Linlithgow, Montrose, Peebles, Perth, Renfrew, Roxburgh, Rutherglen and Stirling. Most of these grew up beside a royal castle. They became centres of the king's government and, you will notice, several have given their names to shires.

Edinburgh below the Castle and the burgh of Canongate outside Holyrood Abbey as they probably looked in 1450. Notice how few houses there were in Canongate

William the Lion was another king who founded many burghs. Burghs of barony which lords created include Prestwick and Kirkintilloch, while Glasgow, St Andrews and Canongate (which was then separate from the royal burgh of Edinburgh) are also burghs of barony, but bishops or abbots gave them their charters.

Although a charter was a sign of a burgh's rights, it could not guarantee that it would prosper. Burghs were, above all, places where people traded, and they would only grow if they were in the right places. Ports like Aberdeen, Dunbar and Irvine flourished by fishing, and Dumfries and Berwick relied on the rich lands around them. Berwick exported most of the wool from the Border abbeys. Stirling grew up where an important route crossed the Forth.

Trades and Trade

The burghs were a new stage in the story of how men made a living. The townspeople did not have to meet all their needs by doing everything for themselves. Some would learn a trade, making something to sell, such as shoes; another might do a service for which people were willing to pay, like shoeing horses. The money they earned gave them freedom to buy what they wanted. Merchants lived completely by trading, that is, by buying goods and selling them at a profit. Towns near castles grew because there were people there with money and expensive tastes. Merchants could always sell wines from France, fine woollen cloth from Flanders, honey, onions, figs and spices such as pepper, cinnamon and nutmeg.

The People in the Burghs

Some families had always lived in the burgh. But if serfs escaped from their lords, and held a piece of land in the burgh and stayed free for a year and a day, they, too, could become burgesses. Men from England or Normandy who were skilled in some craft might be allowed to stay, and there were merchants from Flanders, known as *Flemings*, in places like Berwick and Perth in David I's reign. Later, however, when crafts became organised, members of a trade would not let others with the same trade come in. In the larger towns, especially in the ports, all the merchants joined together in the merchant *gild* which often gained full control of the affairs of the burgh.

Town Councils and Freedom

At first, each burgess paid rent for his own land to the king's officials, but many burghs saw that they stood to gain if they could run their own affairs. A lump sum, paid to the king each year by the burgh as a whole gave them this right. In 1319, for example, the town of Aberdeen paid the king £213.33. Its burgesses became free men and, equally important, the provost and bailies and 'good men of the better, more discreet and more trustworthy of the burgh', whom the burgesses chose, formed the town council. In this way burghs became self-governing and the burgesses free men.

What a Burgh Looked Like

To us the burghs would seem extremely small, more like our present-day villages in size. The townsfolk still relied on the land for much of their food. The town-herd collected their cows early in the morning, drove them out to the common, and brought them back for milking in the late afternoon.

As we approach the burgh, we watch the merchants' servants and others weeding their land on the 'burgh acres', on our way to the East Port. This is one of the gates in the wall around the town. Inside it we come to a wider area, the market place, and there in the middle is the Mercat Cross. This is where the weekly markets are held and proclamations are read, and where strangers pay their dues on being allowed to trade in the town. Nearby is the little parish church. The

This plan of Edinburgh in 1647 gives some idea of how its High Street and closes looked rather like a fish-bone (page 66)

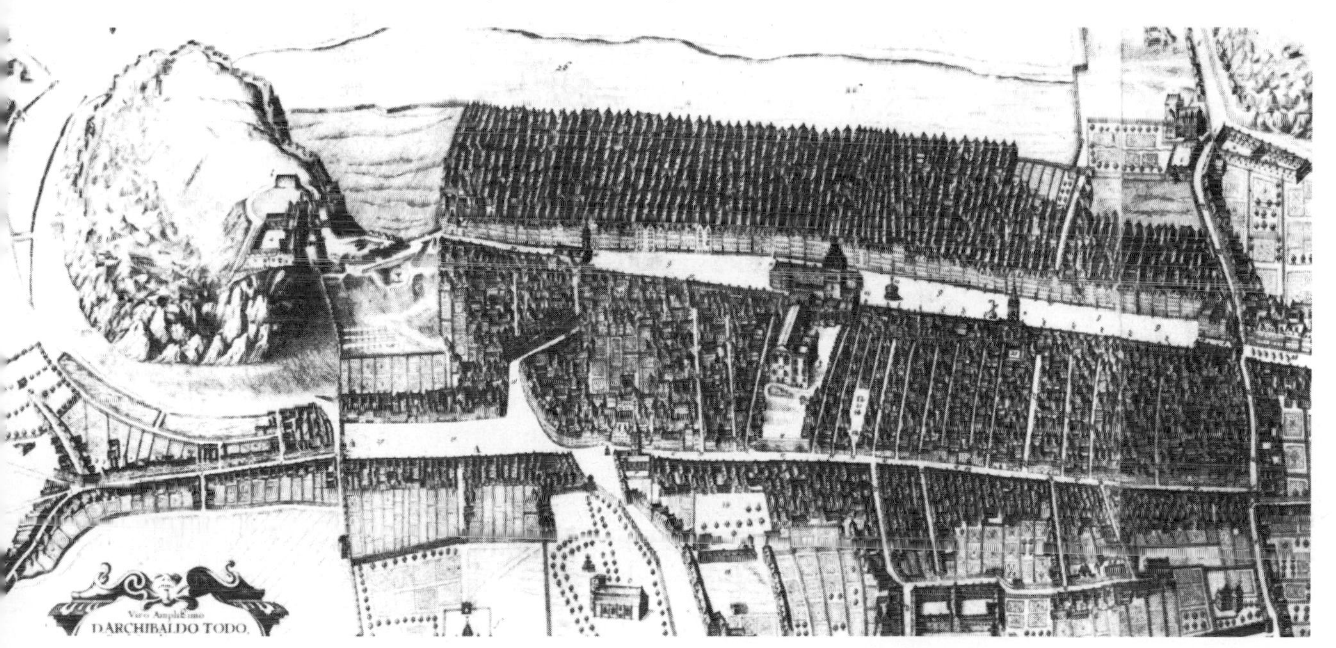

market place narrows at one end into the Hie Gate or High Street. It may be the only street. Notice the cobble stones and the open drains. Piles of filth clutter the street, the place smells. Small wonder that plagues are common!

Mostly built of wood, and with thatched roofs, the little houses line the street. Everyone likes to live in the High Street, so, where a piece of land has been split, we may see two narrow houses with their gable ends to the street. Behind the houses some gardens stretch as far as the burgh wall, but with more people coming and wanting houses, new houses are in side streets or up closes at right angles to the High Street. The burgh has the pattern of a fish-bone with the High Street as the main bone.

Round the burgh is a wall of earth with a palisade on top, to keep people safe. They have weapons in their houses to take with them when it is their turn to go on guard after the gates have been closed for the night. This happens at curfew time, when the bell tolls to warn people to damp down their fires. They are always afraid of fire.

Crafts

People learned crafts or trades of all kinds. There were many *smiths*: blacksmiths, goldsmiths and tinsmiths. Some men were *websters* or weavers, *baxters* or bakers, fleshers, skinners and glovers. Others might be fletchers, lorimers, saddlers, potters, masons and tailors. New jobs meant new surnames. Many of our streets and markets, too, take their names from trades, e.g. Potterrow, Fleshmarket.

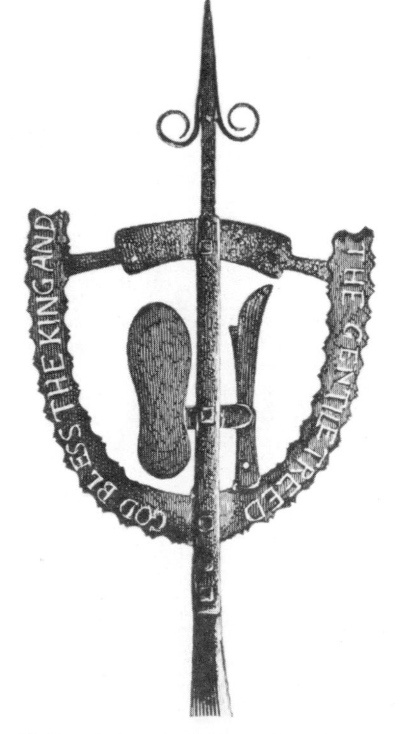

Halberd showing the craft emblem of the souters of Selkirk

To learn the craft of making shoes, a boy had to become an apprentice for seven years. He worked in his master's workshop in part of the house. He had to be careful to obey his master and his master's wife too, for he lived in their house. Gradually he picked up the secrets of the trade and improved his skill until, at the end of his apprenticeship, he became a tradesman or *journeyman* (meaning 'paid by the day', from the French *journée,* day). To become a member of the craft, he had to make his 'masterpiece', a fine pair of shoes. If the deacon of the craft thought this piece of work was good enough, he could set up in business for himself as a master-craftsman. So it was in all the other trades.

Each craft laid down rules for its own members. It limited the number of apprentices a master might employ, fixed wages and prices, set standards of workmanship, and did its best to care for the widows and orphans of its members.

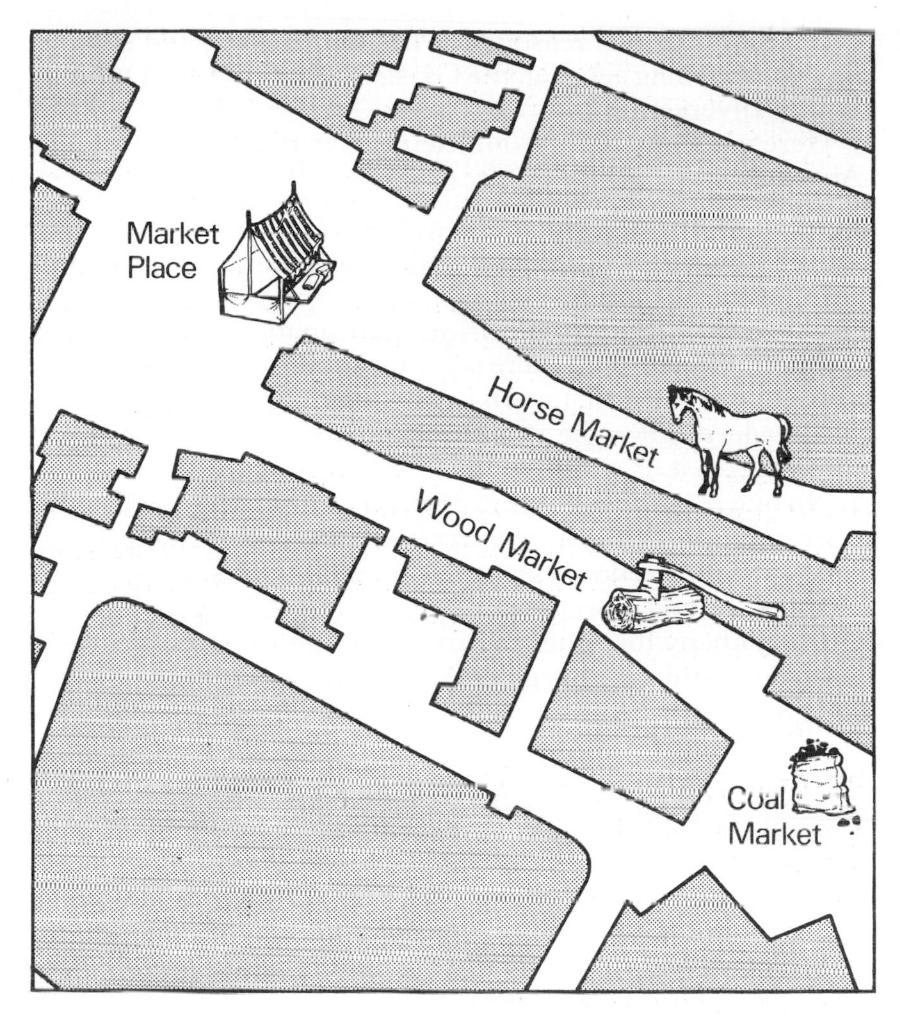

Kelso markets

Markets and Fairs

There were no shops. Buying and selling took place on market days each week at stalls in the market place. Some burghs had special markets, which can be detected from street names. The Haymarket and the Lawnmarket (originally Landmarket, where produce of the land was sold) in Edinburgh, and the Coal, Wood and Horse Markets in Kelso are good examples. Fairs did not happen so often. The right to hold a fair was limited to some royal burghs once or twice a year. The luxuries merchants brought from abroad made the countryfolk stand and stare. Making things in the town stopped; this was the time for selling. Acrobats and minstrels came to entertain in what was the highlight of the year.

Many towns still have holidays and 'all the fun of the fair', even where the real reasons for the fair (buying and selling) disappeared long ago, e.g. the Glasgow Fair, and the Lammas Fair at Inverkeithing.

Here are some rules from the charter the king granted to Aberdeen:

1. I forbid any foreign merchant within the sheriffdom of Aberdeen from buying or selling anything except in my burgh of Aberdeen.
2. Foreign merchants will bring their goods to my burgh of Aberdeen and shall there sell them and pay his penny.
3. No one is to keep a tavern in any town in the sheriffdom of Aberdeen unless he is a knight of the town and residing [living] in it.
4. No one residing outside my burgh of Aberdeen shall make or cause to be made any dyed or mixed cloth within the county of Aberdeen except my burgesses of Aberdeen who are in the gild merchant.
5. I forbid any foreigner to buy or sell hides [skins] or wool except within my burgh of Aberdeen.

Something for You to Do

Use this chapter to learn all you can about your town. For example:

1. *a*) What kind of burgh do you live in, or near? When did it gain its charter? Who granted it?
   b) If you live in an old burgh, why did it grow to start with?
   c) What crafts did men work at? Do any of them survive today?
   d) Does the town still have a fair? What happens at it now? What used to happen?
2. *a*) In an old burgh, go out and draw a plan of the market place, the high street, the old closes and ports. Put in the old parish church and the mercat cross. Try to find a map which will show the boundaries of the town.
   b) See how many names of streets you can find which refer to old trades and markets.
3. Make sure that you understand the following: masterpiece, curfew, 'pay his penny'.
4. Have a close look at the emblem of 'the souters o' Selkirk' to see what they made.
5. Write a description of 'Dawn till dusk in an old Scottish Burgh'.

15 The Monks of Melrose Abbey

Some of the monks David I brought to Scotland were Cistercians, known as 'White Monks' from the cloaks they wore. They had gone back to the simple life laid down by St Benedict, a life of prayer and work.

Benedict and the Rule

Benedict was the son of a rich Roman noble. When he was at school in Rome in the fifth century AD, he was so horrified by the wicked lives most people led that he left home to live as a hermit in a cave. It was common for holy men to turn their backs on the world and go and live in the wilderness alone, but Benedict was not left on his own. He did not want anyone to follow him but men came, men who wanted to give up their lives to God. He taught them how to live together as a band of brothers, calling one another 'brother'. Together they built a great church on the hill called Monte Cassino in Italy.

In the next five hundred years, monasteries [houses for monks] were set up all over western Europe. In Scotland, of course, people knew about St Columba and his followers, but they had been monks of a different kind, who lived in separate huts and wandered from place to place as missionaries, preaching to the people.

Benedict drew up the rules of conduct needed by men who were living together all the time. They had two main duties: to worship God (this took them into Church seven times a day) and to work. In addition, they took three vows:

1. *Poverty*—to give up everything they had
2. *Chastity*—never to marry
3. *Obedience*—to obey the abbot without question.

A Benedictine monk

Monks in Scotland

David I did most to bring bands of monks from England and France to Scotland. His mother, St Margaret, had invited the first monks to Dunfermline. He gave land to the monks, mainly on the lowlands of the south and east. As time went on, barons also gave some of their lands to the abbeys, which became great landowners with some of the best land in

Scotland. Later it was said of David that 'he left the Kirk ower rich and the Crown ower poor'.

There were two main reasons why kings and nobles gave away land like this. The first was that the monks were learned and could do much to improve a backward country. Secondly, people in the Middle Ages were very religious, and they wanted to make sure that when they died they went to Heaven. If they gave lands to an abbey, the monks would pray for their souls.

Monks in Melrose

The first White Monks in Scotland settled at Melrose, on flat land south of the River Tweed. The land was good for growing crops. There were rich meadows for their cows and higher pastures for their sheep. The forest supplied timber for building and fuel. Water from the river drove their corn mill and flushed the great drain which carried waste away from all the buildings. From the slopes of the Eildon hills came a good supply of water, later carried by pipes to the abbey buildings. Good building stone could be quarried nearby.

When they had put up their first simple church, the

Melrose Abbey
(reconstruction by Alan Sorrell)

brothers started to lay out all the other buildings they needed. In course of time, a splendid stone church was built of local stone by bands of masons like those on page 73. They left their marks, cut in the stone on the parts they built.

Gradually the brothers were divided into two types:

1. The *monks*, who took part in all the religious services, and wrote and taught and healed.
2. The *lay brothers*, who did not take full vows, and did most of the heavy work about the abbey and its lands. They lived and slept apart from the monks, and they had their own cloister as well.

If we arrive at the abbey after nine in the morning, we shall meet the monks coming from the church after service. This is their fourth service of the day, the first one having been at midnight. They walk slowly, silently, their heads bowed as they make their way along the cloister walk to the chapter house, where they stand quietly, the tiled floor under their sandalled feet, to hear a portion of the rules read to them and to be told what they are to do that day. Two brothers see that the church is ready for the next service. Brother Reginald goes to make more candles from wax for the altar. Brother John sets to work on his accounts, while the others go off to work in the gardens or study in the cloister. There they can only look inwards, for behind them on all sides walls of stone shut off their eyes and their minds from the world outside.

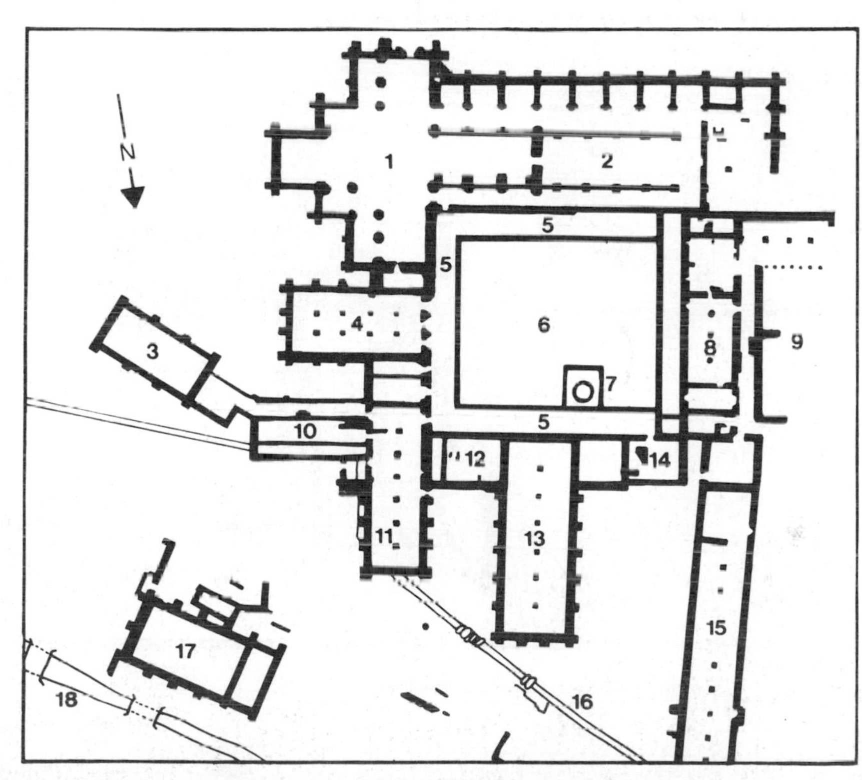

Plan of Melrose Abbey

1 Monks' Choir
2 Nave for Lay Brothers
3 Infirmary
4 Chapter House
5 Cloister
6 Cloister Garden
7 Basin
8 Lay Brothers' Dining Hall
9 Lay Brothers' Cloister
10 Latrines
11 Monks' Dormitory
12 Warming Room
13 Monks' Dining Hall
14 Kitchen
15 Storehouses
16 Great Drain
17 Abbot's Hall
18 Corn Mill Lade

In the stables, the horses are harnessed for a nobleman and his followers. There is the nobleman now with his two sons, saying farewell to the abbot after spending the night in the abbot's hall. As we walk towards the cloister, the voices of the boys or novices ring out clearly as they recite their lessons. Passing the monks' dining hall, we see the nobleman's servants loading their horses with food and baggage for the journey north to spend the night at Newbattle Abbey.

As we go out through the abbey gates, the almoner is giving bread to the poor. A heavily-laden cart creaks as axle and solid wheels all turn together, bringing a load of wood for the kitchen fires. And here, wearing a black cloak and a square black cap, comes a bearded monk, an Austin canon, carrying a message from the Abbot of Jedburgh.

Men were all busy there, getting ready for the next meal, the next service, the next world. But the abbey was not simply a great church where monks lived; it was a great centre of industry. It imported lime from Kelso, lead for roofs from England and oak from Flanders.

Even people living at some distance from Melrose might have been in contact with it through its lands in Berwickshire on the way to the sea, for example, on the uplands of Selkirkshire, Roxburghshire and Peebleshire, in the west at Mauchline, Turnberry and Maybole, or in the towns of Perth, Edinburgh and Berwick where the monks had houses.

Monks in church (from an old book)

Building an abbey

Monks and Farming

The monks were good farmers. This abbey had nine large farms, called granges. They were really villages, with the hovels of the serfs and their families clustering beside the byres, the corn mill and the brew-houses. Usually one of the lay brothers acted as farm steward. At seed time and harvest all the monks went out to help in the fields. They knew how to grow heavy crops of oats, barley, pease and beans.

They cleared much wasteland and put it under the plough. Alexander II, for example, gave them 'my whole waste of Ettrick'. They set their serfs to improve it and before long it was bringing in a rent of £66 a year.

Several of the monks worked in the gardens and orchards, some kept bees for their honey (there was no sugar in Scotland in the Middle Ages) and some went fishing. The abbey had many of the finest stretches of water in the Tweed, and the monks must have eaten many a meal of trout and salmon.

They were great breeders of animals. Many oxen were needed for pulling ploughs and carts. Cows and goats were kept for their milk, some of which was made into butter and cheese. The abbey owned hundreds of horses; it is reckoned that at one time it had as many as 1400. This reminds us how important the horse was in the Middle Ages, for carrying men and goods in peace and war. The monks must also have been among the first horse-dealers.

They were most famous, however, for breeding sheep. Sheep were very small and scraggy then and were kept mainly for their soft wool. They were moved up to high pastures in summer and to the lower slopes about September. Roads were so poor that carts could not go far. The fleeces were carried by pack-horses, or on sledges pulled by horses, down the slopes of the Cheviots and Lammermuirs to the abbey, and along the valley to the port of Berwick. There the monks had storehouses, where the wool was kept for ships to carry it to Flanders where it was made into fine cloth.

The wool trade made the abbey wealthy. It helped the king and country, too, for the king received customs duties from the wool which was exported, and the sale of wool brought money into the country.

When you visit an old abbey, try to see the ruined walls raised up into the complete buildings they once were. Remember, the whole settlement was a place where monks prayed and worked for centuries. Think too, of the men who built such huge and fine buildings to the glory of God so long ago.

Something for You to Do

1. What were a monk's two main duties?
2. *a*) Draw a plan of Melrose Abbey.
   b) Mark in each part and say what it was used for.
3. How did the abbey help *a*) the people, and *b*) the country?
4. Describe the scene on page 73.
5. Imagine that you live in the country in the Middle Ages, and that a band of monks has come to build an abbey nearby. Write what you think about their coming and what they are doing.
6. In David I's reign, the monks at Melrose fed 4000 starving people for three months when there was a famine. Write a short play about this for the class to act.

16 The Struggle for Independence

1. Under William Wallace

In the end, my friends,
We've nane but the folk; they've nocht [nothing]
To loss [lose] but life and libertie
But gin [if] we've thame, we've aa. They're Scotland
Nane ither.

Sydney Goodsir Smith, *The Wallace*

You can see this statue of William Wallace on your way in to Edinburgh Castle

The life of the ordinary man working on the land may strike us as humdrum and hopeless, but there was the occasional holiday [holy day] to enjoy, and the hope of a happier life in Heaven. Though he might not notice it in the reign of Alexander III (1249–86), the country was becoming prosperous. People obeyed the king's laws for he kept a firm hold on the land. More burghs were founded, and trade increased, especially through Berwick. More and more serfs were gaining their freedom. Farming was flourishing under the guiding hand of the monks. The Vikings, who had been defeated at *Largs* in 1263 by storms, disease and Alexander's forces, agreed to hand over the Hebrides to Scotland and to leave the country alone. Scotland was at peace with her southern neighbour. It was an age of peace and prosperity, a 'golden age'.

When the king's dead body was found on the shore near Kinghorn in 1286 this happy period in our history came suddenly to an end. He left no son to succeed him; the heiress was a little girl, Margaret, the 'Maid of Norway'. When she died in Orkney, Scotland was left without a ruler. The men who claimed the crown might have gathered their men and started to fight each other. Instead, they looked to Edward I of England to choose the next king.

Edward had recently conquered the Welsh and built strong castles to keep the peace in Wales, and he dreamed of the whole island being brought under his control. First, he insisted that the claimants recognise him as overlord of Scotland, and then, by the Award of Berwick, he gave the throne to John Balliol who had the best claim.

John Balliol as King

King John ruled like a puppet because Edward pulled the strings. Edward took every chance to show that he was overlord of Scotland, even summoning John to England to pay a wine bill Alexander III owed. When he demanded that the Scots should provide men and money for an English war against France, Edward went too far. Scotsmen had never been forced to fight abroad even for their own king. A council of barons decided to make an alliance with France against their common enemy, Edward I. This Franco-Scottish alliance of 1295, later called the *Auld Alliance*, was to draw both countries together and see Scots and French fighting together against England until the time of Mary, Queen of Scots.

A Scottish raid into England drew the full force of Edward's anger. With a strong army, he captured Berwick and put so many men, women and children in it to the sword that the streets streamed with blood. At Dunbar the Scottish army was defeated, and Balliol soon had to surrender.

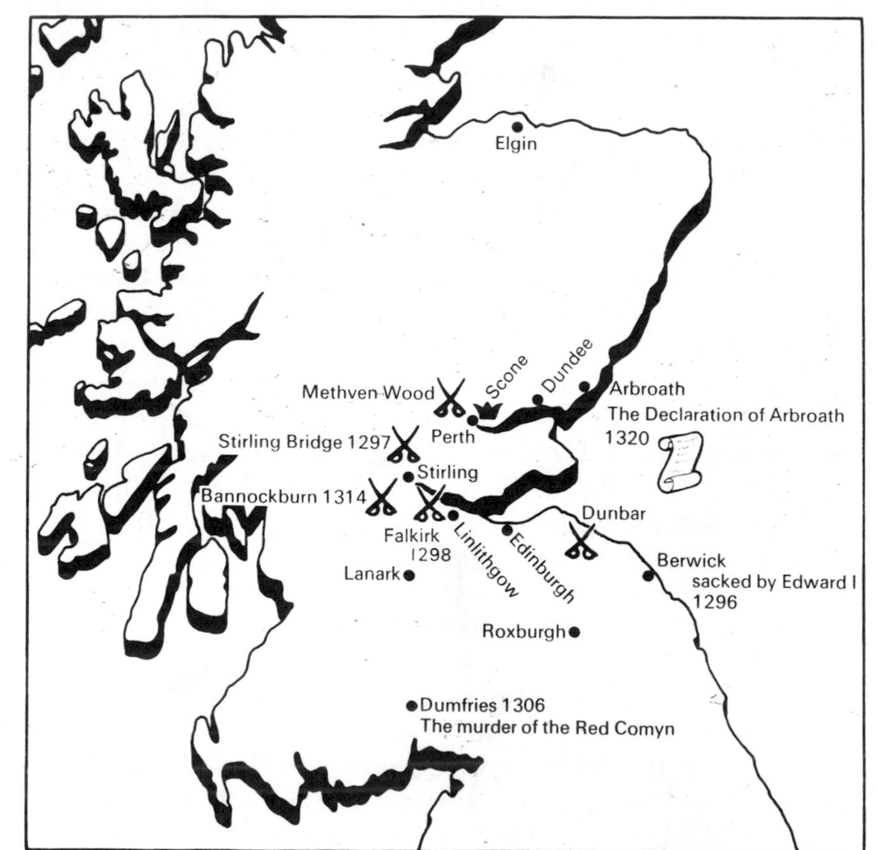

Scotland during the Wars of Independence

Edward's men marched as far north as Elgin. English nobles took charge of the country, and English troops filled the castles. They took away the Stone of Destiny from Scone, where it had been used to instal Scottish kings, and put it in the coronation chair in Westminster Abbey. The Holy Rood of St Margaret, said to be part of Christ's Cross, and the bulk of the Scottish records of state, were also taken south. Edward seemed to have Scotland in his power.

The Fight for Freedom

Although most of the nobles had sworn oaths of homage to Edward, few other people welcomed the English soldiers or were willing to pay taxes to the English. The nation's hour of need produced the leaders it required, and people began to fight back in several places. 'Ane nobil young man, callit William Wallace inspyrit by God,' a Scottish writer tells us, 'tuik pairt with the puir pepill and defendit the realm.' Wallace was not one of the great nobles, but a knight's son from Elderslie in Renfrewshire. He had reason to hate the English. After he had slain an English soldier in a quarrel they killed his wife in Lanark and burned his house. In his fury Wallace led a raid against the English in Lanark and killed Hazelrig, the English sheriff, with his own sword. News of this spread the spirit of rebellion. His band of followers became an army as the common folk flocked to join him. He was a local hero, soon to become a great patriot determined to free his country from the invaders. But a man who is a hero to his fellow-countrymen may be regarded quite differently by his enemies. The monks in a priory just south of the Border wrote this opinion of him in their chronicle:

'A certain bloody man, William Wallace, who before that had been the leading bandit in Scotland . . . induced the poor people to gather to his aid.'

Meanwhile another knight's son, Andrew of Moray, was driving the English out of the castles in the north. When Wallace was attacking Dundee in 1297, he heard that an English army was marching north towards Stirling. Andrew of Moray and his men joined him. They made for Stirling and waited in a strong position covering the wooden bridge across the Forth. The bridge was so narrow that men could cross only two or three abreast, but the English began to go over. When about half of them were across, and waiting to re-form their ranks, Wallace sounded his horn for the attack.

The Scots charged with their spears, and captured the end of the bridge. The English who had crossed could not retreat. They perished on the field of battle or in the river. The remainder, who could not cross to help them, were unwilling spectators on the south bank, and then they turned and fled.

Wallace drove the English out of the south-east of the country. Scotland was free, and Wallace and Andrew of Moray were able to show their authority by inviting the merchants of Lubeck and Hamburg to come to Scotland to trade again. But the country was suffering from famine, because of all the fighting. Wallace led an expedition into England, which drove Edward to collect another army and follow the Scots back into Scotland. He caught them and defeated them at *Falkirk* in 1298. The courage and spears of the Scots were no match for the charges by the English cavalry or the arrows showered down on them. Scotland suffered a serious defeat and Edward had proved himself the 'Hammer of the Scots'.

Having lost the battle, Wallace kept on trying to set the country free. English troops were everywhere, trying to put down local risings. It seemed to Edward that his grip on Scotland would not be tight until Wallace was his prisoner. At last Wallace was tricked by Sir John Menteith, a Scottish knight, who took him prisoner at Robroyston near Glasgow and handed him over to Edward. Wallace was taken to London, tried for treason to a king he did not recognise and condemned to a horrible death. He died for Scotland.

Something for You to Do

1. Give three reasons why people have looked back on the reign of Alexander III as 'The Golden Age of Scottish History'.
2. *a*) Why was Edward I interested in Scotland?
   b) Why did the Scots make an alliance with France in 1295?
   c) Who gave Wallace and Andrew of Moray more support, the nobles or the common people?
3. Read again the two opinions of William Wallace. What do you think of him?
4. On a map of central Scotland insert the places named in the chapter. Use signs like ⚔ = Battle.
5. Imagine that you are a war correspondent of a newspaper. Write an eye-witness account of the Battle of Stirling.

17 The Struggle for Independence

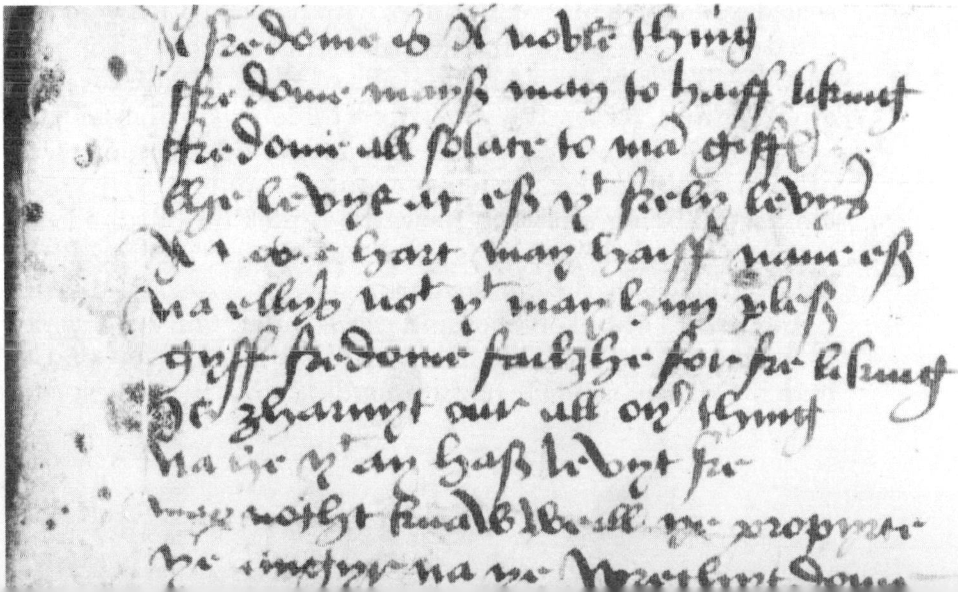

(Top) Robert the Bruce. Statue on the way in to Edinburgh Castle
(Bottom) An example of fourteenth-century handwriting from *The Brus* by John Barbour, to compare with the four lines at the top of the page

2. *Under Robert the Bruce*

> Ah Freedom is a noble thing!
> Freedom makes man to have liking [pleasure];
> Freedom all solace [comfort] to man gives;
> He lives at ease that freely lives!
>
> John Barbour, *The Brus*

Any hope of Scotland regaining her freedom must have died almost completely when news came that Wallace was dead. English soldiers living in every castle and burgh were signs to the Scottish people that Edward was their lord. The land was bare and food was scarce. But within a year the Scots had a new leader, a man of rank who was prepared to give up his English lands to fight for Scotland's freedom. He was descended from the Norman to whom David I had given Annandale, and he had a strong right to be king. His name was Robert the Bruce.

To rid Scotland of the English was difficult enough, but Bruce added to his difficulties. In 1306, at the Grey Friars' Church in Dumfries, he met his rival for the crown, John Comyn (the 'Red Comyn'). They quarrelled, Bruce wounded Comyn with his dagger and, as he rushed out to confess that he had disturbed the peace of a holy place, his friends went in and killed the wounded man. Comyn's men became his deadly foes, and the Church regarded him as a murderer and an enemy of God.

Robert the Bruce
(from his seal)

To win support now, he needed to be king. He was made king in secret at Scone; few bishops came because of the ban of the Church on Bruce.

King or Not

Robert the Bruce might now call himself Robert I, King of Scotland, but he was a king hunted in his own country. A defeat by the English in Methven Wood near Perth was followed by another in the west at the hands of the Red Comyn's relatives. He was forced to leave the mainland altogether for a time. When he returned to Ayrshire with a small band of desperate men, he used the tactics of a guerrilla fighter, raiding and ambushing the enemy, but avoiding open battles against larger numbers than his own. He and his men 'lived off the land'. They carried only little bags of oatmeal to make oatcakes; they hunted deer and killed cattle and sheep to feed themselves.

When Edward I, the 'Hammer of the Scots', died Bruce's task was easier because his son, Edward II, was not a soldier like his father. This gave Bruce the chance of dealing with his Scottish enemies. He conquered Aberdeenshire, Argyll and Galloway ('the Comyn countries') and had the north of Scotland strongly behind him.

Capturing Castles

At last Bruce could turn on his English foes, the soldiers holding the Scottish castles. Though he took many of the smaller towers quite easily, he did not have the kind of heavy siege-engines needed to capture stone castles by direct attack. He had to use his eyes to detect weaknesses in their defences, and his wits to trick the enemy. Often his men scaled walls by using rope ladders with hooks, which could be lifted up on the points of their spears to catch the top of a castle wall. They climbed the walls of Perth Castle this way after wading across the moat in winter up to the neck in water; Linlithgow was captured by men hidden under a load of hay; Roxburgh by Sir James Douglas's men wearing dark cloaks and being mistaken for cattle; and Edinburgh Castle by Sir Thomas Randolph's men who daringly climbed the cliffs of the castle rock in the dark.

Edward II's hold on Scotland was slender. Only the castles at Bothwell and Stirling held out for him, and he had to march north at once. He had a splendid army, the largest ever to invade Scotland up to that time. 20 000 there were, raising the dust on the road north to Stirling, their main strength lying in the long column of heavily-armoured knights on horseback. The Scots had only 6 000 men altogether and only a few were horsemen and archers. When the Scottish scouts looked out on the enemy and picked out the longbowmen and plumed horsemen, they must have wondered, 'Will this be a defeat like Falkirk, all over again?'

The Battle of Bannockburn, 1314

But Bruce's men were in a good position on the wooded ground of New Park. Protected to the south by the bog, and by the pits which his men had dug near the Bannock Burn as traps for the English horses, they blocked the road to Stirling Castle. Edward must either attack the Scots in the wood, where his cavalry would be hampered, or else take the low road across the marsh between New Park and the Forth. On the afternoon of 23rd June, the English cavalry tried a direct attack on the Scots in the wood, but some floundered in the pits and the rest withdrew. The English knight, De Bohun, charged the king and Bruce felled him at the cost of his good battle-axe.

Edward's army crossed the Bannock Burn and camped for the night. In one sense, the water protected them; in another sense, they were in a trap. When the sun came up, columns of Scottish spearmen advanced boldly down the slope, then

Plan of Battle of Bannockburn

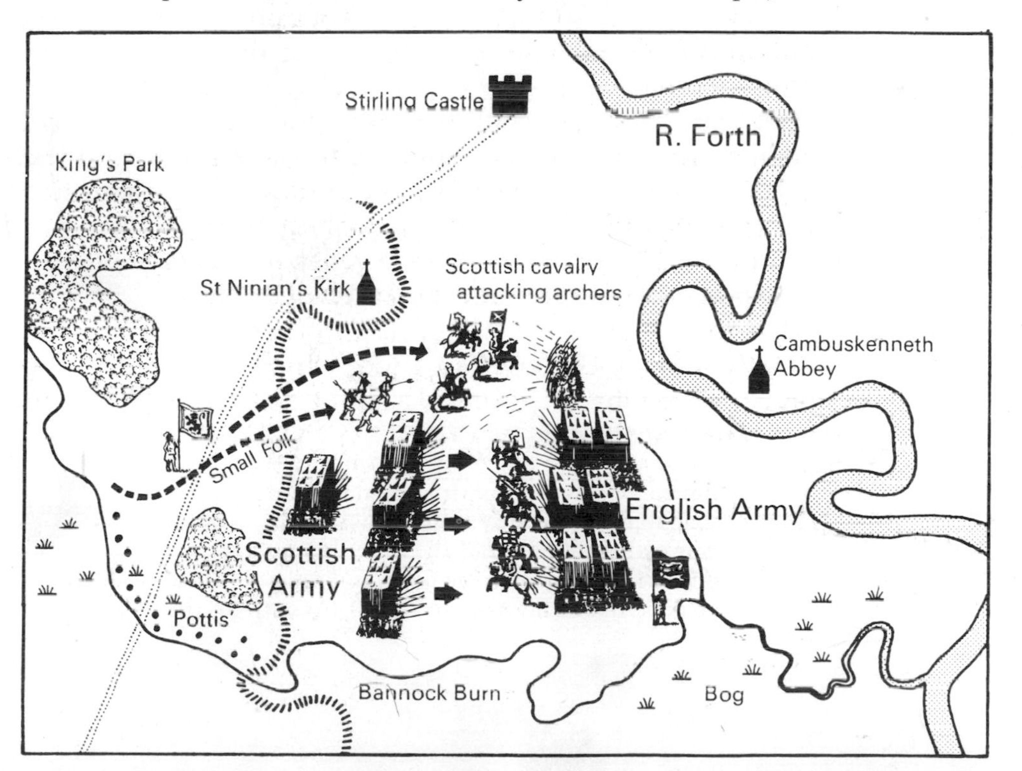

The sacred box, or reliquary, which once held relics of St Columba

stopped and knelt in prayer. A sacred box of the relics of St Columba was held up before them. They believed it would help them to win.

'See,' said Edward, 'they kneel to ask for mercy.'

'Yes, sire, but not from you,' said a knight near him. 'It is God's mercy that they seek. These men will conquer or die.'

Edward could not believe it. Here came Scottish foot-soldiers in columns, their spears thrust out like the prickles of a hedgehog, daring to attack English knights and bowmen. A counter-attack by the English cavalry crumbled before the Scottish spears; a word from Bruce and his horsemen routed the English archers; this certainly would not be the battle of Falkirk over again. But the battle was not yet won. The English had far more men and equipment, but they had no room to spread out on a wide front. The fighting was desperate, hand-to-hand. You could hear the clang of sword on armour, the splintering of wood, the mad gallop of riderless horses, the shouting, the moans of dying men. The battle was confused, but the English were trapped with water at their backs.

Probably by Bruce's orders, the 'small folk', the armed farmers and camp-followers, left their shelter in the valley and came to the field of battle.

'On them', they shouted, 'On them! They fail!' Their arrival encouraged the Scots; they seemed like a fresh army to the English who broke and fled. The Forth swallowed many an English knight. An early writer tells us that, 'Bannockburn was so full of bodies that on top of drowned horses and men, men could pass over it dryshod [without getting their feet wet].'

The battle of Bannockburn, on 24th June 1314, was Scotland's greatest victory. Much booty was taken, and the English surrendered Stirling Castle. For several years raids into the north of England were made until independence was won and the English signed the *Treaty of Northampton* in 1328. Scotland was a free and separate kingdom.

What the Scots had been fighting for is best described in the *Declaration of Arbroath* in 1320, which they sent to the Pope, asking him to recognise Robert I as king of an independent Scotland.

> For so long as one hundred men remain alive, we shall never under any conditions submit to the domination of the English. It is not for glory or riches or honour that we fight, but only for liberty, which no good man will consent to lose but with his life.

Bruce's Heart

Bruce had saved Scotland and made its people a nation. But could he save his own soul? As long as the ban of the Church was on him, he could not be buried as a Christian and believed he had no prospect of reaching Heaven. At length, worn down by his labours and very ill, he heard the good news that the Pope recognised him as king and as a faithful member of the Church. He was never able to go on a crusade as he had wished, but he made Sir James Douglas, 'the good Sir James', promise to carry his heart, enclosed in a casket, to the Holy Land after his death.

For the past two hundred years, Christian knights from many nations had fought in the Crusades or 'Wars of the Cross', to free Palestine from the Mohammedan Turks who had conquered it. Few Scots had gone there to fight, because they were needed to defend their own country against England. Sir James Douglas and his companions, however, set out and fought against the Mohammedans in Spain. There, in the thick of the battle, Douglas and his followers were killed. Bruce's heart was returned safely to Scotland and placed in Melrose Abbey.

Something for You to Do

1. *a*) Give two reasons why the Comyns fought against Bruce.
   b) Why did Bruce not want to fight big battles against the English?
2. Fill in the places named in this chapter on the map you made for the last chapter. Use the sign ▀ = Castle.
3. Which of the castles captured by Bruce's men is nearest to your home? The capture of the castles is thrilling reading, either in Sir Walter Scott's *Tales of a Grandfather* or in H.W. Meikle's *Story of Scotland.*
4. *a*) Give three reasons for the Scottish victory at Bannockburn.
   b) For an 'eye-witness' account of Bannockburn read *I was at Bannockburn* by Agnes Mure Mackenzie.
5. Copy down carefully the quotation from the Declaration of Arbroath. The words are worth learning.
6. In groups find out more about the Crusades. Here are some suggested topics: Mohammed, Mohammedanism, the Koran, Richard I, Saladin. A good story about the Crusades is *Knight Crusader* by Ronald Welch.

18 The Later Middle Ages

This is my country,
The land that begat me.
These windy spaces
Are surely my own,
And those who here toil
In the sweat of their faces
Are flesh of my flesh
And bone of my bone.
Sir Alexander Gray: *Scotland*

The Wars of Independence were Scotland's moment of glory when the people felt they had become a nation. But the price of victory was heavy. They had tried their hardest to win against a great and wealthy neighbour, and most of the battles had been fought on Scottish soil. People and beasts, burghs and touns, castles and kirks, had all suffered heavily, and the men who fought for Bruce had to rebuild what had been knocked down.

We do not know how many people were living in Scotland then. Probably there were about 400000 in all in Bruce's time. This is less than the population of Edinburgh in the second half of the twentieth century. Famine and fighting always kept the numbers down, but in 1349–50 a great plague struck the country. This was the *Black Death*, which had already killed millions in Europe. It spread from England into Scotland, where people called it 'the Foul Death of the English'. Many people in Scotland died: we do not know the number but it may have been as many as 100000, or one person out of every four.

More Wars

After the Wars of Independence the country needed a period of peace under a strong king. But when Robert the Bruce died, he was succeeded by a boy, David II. England under Edward III was still the 'Auld Enemy', and defeated the Scots whenever she liked.

English troops marched north in 1333 in the hope of capturing Berwick, Scotland's busiest seaport. Edward's archers slaughtered the Scottish army at the battle of *Halidon Hill*, and then took Berwick and held it for a time. Soon

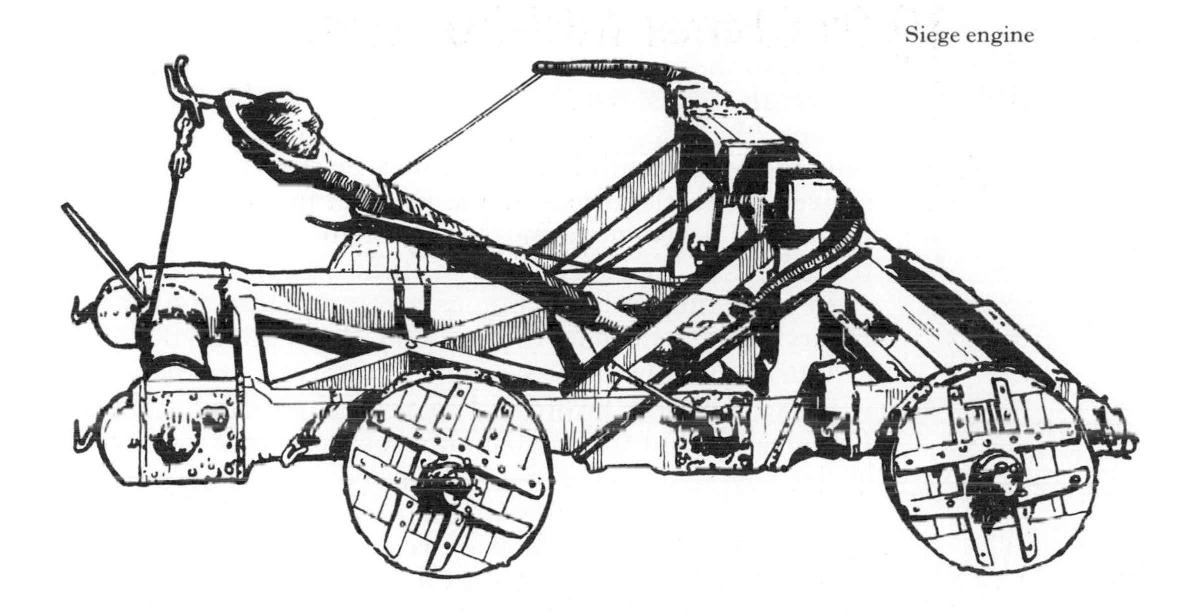

Siege engine

Scotland suffered more burning and killing. Even towns in the north such as Elgin and Aberdeen were burned, and some of the castles which Bruce's men had destroyed were built up again and filled with English troops.

No great Scottish patriot rose up against the invaders, but a woman defied them. She was the Countess of March (known as 'Black Agnes' because of her dark skin), the daughter of Randolph who had captured Edinburgh Castle for Bruce, and she held the castle of Dunbar against an English siege. When the English siege-engines hurled stones at the walls, she and her maids went out with cloths to wipe away the dust. As the months passed, food became so scarce in the castle that it seemed that she would have to surrender. But a brave man, Alexander Ramsay, brought in food by night from the Bass Rock. Black Agnes mockingly sent some of it as a gift to the English commander, and in disgust he gave up trying to capture the castle.

Fortunately for Scotland, Edward needed most of his soldiers elsewhere. In 1339 he attacked France, in what was to become the *Hundred Years War*. By the 'Auld Alliance', the Scots were still expected to make raids on the north of England. In one raid south of the Tyne they were defeated at *Neville's Cross* (1346). Wounded in the face by an arrow, David II was taken prisoner. His ransom cost £66 000, a crippling sum for a poor country.

This figure of Bricius MacKinnon in Iona shows what a fourteenth-century knight looked like

Robert II became king in 1371. His claim to the throne was sound, for he was the son of Walter the Steward and Marjory Bruce, the eldest daughter of Robert I. At the age of 55 he became the first of the Stewart line of Kings. He tried to remain at peace with England, but over 1000 French knights arrived in Scotland to raid the English in 1385. The attack failed, and the enemy came north and burned Edinburgh and the abbeys of Melrose and Dryburgh.

In 1388 the Earl of Douglas advanced into the lands of Henry Percy in the north of England. Percy attacked Douglas at *Otterburn*. The armies fought on fiercely by moonlight, with axe and spear, sword and dagger. Three times wounded, Douglas fell, but the English did not know that the Scottish leader was dying. The Scots attacked, shouting 'Douglas! Douglas!' and drove the English from the field. Douglas died, but he had won as he had dreamed he would, according to the old ballad, *The Battle of Otterbourne*:

> I saw a dead man win a fight,
> And I think that man was I.

Kings and Barons

Kings of Scotland 1329–1488	
David II 1329–71	James I 1406–37
Robert II 1371–90	James II 1437–60
Robert III 1390–1406	James III 1460–88

After the Wars of Independence Robert I took lands away from the barons who had fought against him and gave them to men who had served him well. This made some families very powerful, but there was no danger in this as long as he was king. After Robert I, however, Scotland was unfortunate in her kings. David II was only five when he became king and later was held prisoner in England for eleven years; Robert II, the first of the Stewarts, was too old; his son Robert III was a kind man, but weak; then James I was absent for eighteen years, a prisoner in England. For almost a century (1329–1424) no king had the money, or the men or the will-power to rule Scotland firmly from the centre.

Under a weak or absent king, the heads of big landed families ruled in their own areas as if *they* were kings. Their relatives supported them and lower families in the area found it wise to join them as well. It gave them protection but it added to the number of armed men a great lord could command. Some lords, especially the Earls of Douglas, became very powerful. Other important families were the Crawfords, the Gordons, the Ogilvies, the Lindsays, the Hamiltons, the Homes and later in the south-west, the Kennedys,

> Frae Wigton to the toon o' Ayr
> Port Patrick to the Cruives o' Cree,
> Nae man wad think to bide there
> Unless he coort wi' Kennedy.

It was very difficult to make people take heed of laws in the Highlands. As soon as Robert III, a gentle crippled old man, became king in 1390, his own brother Alexander, known as the 'Wolf of Badenoch', started to cause trouble in the north. With a band of 'wild, wikkit hielandmen', he raided the lands of the Bishop of Moray and burned down his cathedral at Elgin. In other places, clan fights took place often and the king could not stop them. At a clan fight in Perth, Robert III was a helpless spectator as thirty champions from each of the two clans Chattan and Kay fought each other with axe, sword and dagger until nearly all were slain.

Such troubled times drove the king to send his son James to France for safety, but the boy might have been safer at home. His ship was captured by the English, and he was held prisoner in England.

When his father died, *regents* ruled in young James' place. The Lord of the Isles was the master of all the lands in the west from Kintyre in Argyll to the Isle of Lewis in the north, and he made treaties with England as if he were a king. In 1411, Donald, the second Lord of the Isles, led an army of Highlanders across towards Aberdeen. He claimed that the earldom of Ross in the north was his, and was ready to fight for it. At *Harlaw* his army was driven off by spearmen from Buchan and Angus under the Earl of Mar, who were supported by burgesses from Aberdeen. Many were killed on both sides,

> And Hieland and Lowland may mournful be
> For the sair field of Harlaw.

A battle like this shows how much Scotland needed a king who could stop one baron, or one group of men, from fighting another.

James I

Kings Who Tried Hard

James I

When James I returned from England in 1424, he showed that he was that kind of king. He was manly and intelligent, and said he would make Scotland so law-abiding that the key would be enough 'to keep the castle and the bracken-bush the cow.' He called parliaments to help him (from the French word *parler*, to speak), to which representatives of the Church and the burghs came along with the barons. Parliament's job was to agree to taxes and to make laws. For example, Parliament ordered every man to have the proper weapons for a man of his rank and to practise with the bow and arrow in case he was called to fight for the king. Barons were ordered not to have too many armed followers when they rode about the country, and were not to make private wars on one another.

James acted swiftly against the barons and chiefs, who had not been used to having to obey a strong king. He captured his cousin, the Duke of Albany, who had been regent when James was in England, and had him executed at Stirling. In 1428 James ordered the Highland chiefs to meet him in Inverness. He threw over forty in prison, including the Lord of the Isles, and put the most dangerous of them to death. Measures like these did not make Highlanders feel that James was a good king.

A few nobles plotted to kill him when he was staying at the Blackfriars in Perth in 1437. He was warned that he was in danger but he paid no attention. One evening when he was talking with the queen and her ladies, there was a clink of weapons outside. James was unarmed and it was discovered that the door could not be closed. Katherine Douglas, one of the queen's attendants, we are told, used her arm to bar the door while the king escaped through the floorboards to the drains below. Her arm was broken as the armed men burst in. The king was nowhere to be found and the plotters departed. Something, probably a noise, called them back. They noticed the loose boards and plunged down. James was trapped and murdered.

James II, on a monument beside Dryburgh Abbey, carved in the 1790s

James II

James II was crowned at Holyrood when he was only six. The king's guardians, Crichton and Livingston, were frightened of what the other barons would do. They invited the young Earl of Douglas, the most powerful of them, and his brother to come to Edinburgh to visit the king. They came and were entertained to dinner. Then the head of a black bull was placed on the table: it was a sign of death. Young James protested but his guests were hustled off and put to death.

When James II became a man, he tried to be a strong king like his father. He was guided by Bishop Kennedy of St Andrews. Parliament supported him and so did the Church but he knew that he would not be the real king until he proved that he was stronger than the Douglas family. When he discovered that the new Earl of Douglas had made an agreement to join with other earls, he ordered him to come to Stirling Castle, promising that no harm would come to him. James told him bluntly that this league of barons must be broken up at once. Douglas defied him, and James drew his dagger and stabbed him. This action by the king stung the Douglases into rebellion. On Kennedy's advice, James was careful to take on Douglas's allies one at a time. Then, advancing into the Douglas lands, he knocked down their castles and took back all their lands for himself. The power of the Douglases was at an end. This king had shown that he was mightier than any baron.

James II's reign ended in tragedy. He was one of the first to use cannon to blast holes in the castles of barons who would not obey him, and he was the king who brought from Belgium the great cannon called Mons Meg, now in Edinburgh Castle. James was using cannon to try to win back Roxburgh Castle from the English, but when he was watching one of them being fired in 1460, it blew up and killed him.

James III

Once again the new king was only a boy. In 1469 he married Margaret, daughter of the king of Denmark, who was to bring him a large sum of money as her dowry. When this dowry was not paid Orkney and Shetland passed to the Scottish crown instead.

James III was not a man-of-action like his father and grandfather. He trusted no one, not even his own brothers. He was either too lazy or too frightened to govern and did not trouble to travel about the country to see that justice was done. He was not hard enough on the nobles who kept quarrelling with one another. Later they turned against him and would not even fight for him against the English. When he was assembling men to defend the port of Berwick against English invaders, they captured him at Lauder and held him prisoner for a time in Edinburgh. No Scottish army marched to save Berwick, which has been an English town ever since.

Powerful nobles rose against him again in 1488. They had his fifteen year-old son, James, with them calling himself 'Prince of Scotland', and said they fought in his name. Father and son and their two armies faced each other in battle at *Sauchieburn* near Stirling. Thrown from his horse, James III was carried to a corn mill. Thinking he was going to die, he asked for a priest. He was stabbed there by a dagger in an unknown hand.

Something for You to Do

1. Why were these important: the Black Death, the Lordship of the Isles, Parliament?
2. Which family was powerful in your district at this time? Are any of its castles or towers still standing? Find out all you can about it.
3. *a*) Why has the stone carver put a cannon and cannonballs on the memorial to James II on page 89?
   b) Why did none of these James's die in his bed?
4. On a time chart for the period 1329–1488 put in the rulers and main events.

19 The Age of Discovery

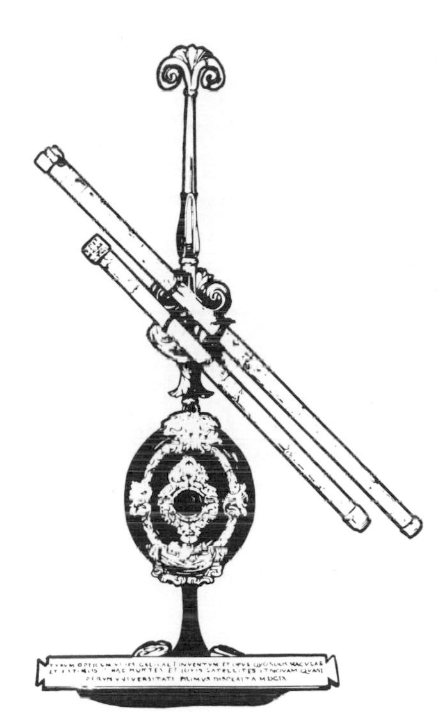

Galileo's telescopes
and lens on display

It is impossible to say exactly when a boy becomes a youth or when a youth becomes a man. In the same way, we know that one age in history differs from the age before it, but we cannot say exactly when the new age begins.

The Middle Ages, the period we have been studying, was the time when the Pope was recognised as God's representative on earth and every Christian looked to him for guidance. Inside each country, on the other hand, a man's position depended on the land he held. Thus, the priest in his church and the lord in his castle were the two great authorities whom everyone believed and obeyed. Churchmen were the only educated men, and people were brought up to believe what they said. 'What do the scholars say?' people asked. 'These things we must learn and believe.'

In the fourteenth and fifteenth centuries, peoples' ideas began to change. They were no longer satisfied with what somebody told them to believe. They began to ask questions, not about the next world but about the world around them. They became curious about its shape and its size, and about the stars and the planets. They also wanted to experiment, to prove things for themselves. To find the truth became a quest; it was the real way to learn. This new age was called the *Renaissance*, meaning the rebirth of enthusiasm for learning.

The Renaissance

The Renaissance began in Italy, in cities like Florence and Venice where merchants came into contact with the ideas of foreign lands in the course of trade. The people in Italy could see around them ruins that reminded them that ancient Rome had been a great civilisation. Perhaps thinkers in early Greece and Rome had known more about the world than they did. Gradually manuscripts written in Greek were brought to Italy where they were eagerly studied. This trickle of documents became a flood when the Turks captured Constantinople in 1453 and Greek scholars living there fled to the West. Those who settled in Italy brought their valuable manuscripts with them.

John Gutenberg, inventor of the printing press

New discoveries were made in science. As early as the thirteenth century, Roger Bacon knew about gunpowder, which, when used in pistols and cannon, was to blast the armoured knight and the castle from the thoughts of military men. A king who had artillery at his command could keep his barons in order. Copernicus, a Polish astronomer, discovered that the earth was not fixed but moved round the sun. Galileo, the Italian scientist, first used the telescope to support the ideas of Copernicus. In another experiment, he dropped stones of different sizes from the top of the leaning tower of Pisa, and proved that they fell at the same rate even though some were heavy and some were light. Leonardo da Vinci, artist, architect, town-planner, sculptor and engineer (perhaps the man of greatest all-round ability) foresaw the aeroplane and the 'covered chariot' (the tank).

In the Middle Ages, students spoke Latin and travelled about Europe to study under great teachers in the universities. Now many were attracted to Italy to study Greek. When they returned home to Germany, France, the Netherlands and Britain, they carried their craze for learning with them.

In Germany, the printing press was invented by John Gutenberg, and in 1476 William Caxton set up his press in England. Following the discovery by the Arabs of a cheap way of making paper, it became possible to produce books in large numbers. By the year 1500, there were nine million printed books in Europe, compared with about 100 000 written by hand in the whole of the Middle Ages. More people learned to read and write and so to find things out for themselves.

Other men felt the urge to create. Some were great artists, such as Leonardo da Vinci, who painted the 'Mona Lisa'. Some were architects who went back to the Greeks for inspiration. They tried to make their buildings in proportion, so that their breadth and height were 'just right'. They gave up building arches and built doorways and windows with lintels over them, as we do today; and some of their new buildings had columns and domes. St Peter's Church in Rome, and St Paul's Cathedral in London which Sir Christopher Wren rebuilt in the seventeenth century, have many of these new features.

Leonardo da Vinci

Leonardo da Vinci's idea of how a tank would look

Voyages of Discovery

People wanted to find out about other lands. The world they

knew in the Middle Ages was small. It consisted of Europe and the lands round the Mediterranean, to which Arab traders brought the wealth of the East from India, China and the Indies which people called the Spice Islands. It was possible to explore once sailors had the compass to guide them.

Prince Henry of Portugal, known as the Navigator, encouraged his sea-captains to sail farther and farther south along the coast of Africa. Following them, Bartholomew Diaz reached the Cape of Good Hope in 1488 and then Vasco da Gama sailed round the Cape and crossed the Indian Ocean, and in 1498 he arrived in India. This was to be the route sailors took to the East until the Suez Canal was opened in 1869.

But if the world is round, why not reach India by sailing west? In 1492 Christopher Columbus, a sailor from Genoa, sailed west with three ships Isabella, the Queen of Spain had given him. Weeks on the open sea terrified his men but Columbus kept them going. At last they reached land, one of a group of islands which included Cuba and Haiti. Columbus thought they were the Spice Islands and called them *Indies*. On later voyages he touched the mainland. This was not Asia, as he had hoped, but South America. Other captains sailed west. John Cabot found Newfoundland and claimed it for England, Amerigo Vespucci, whose name was given to America, explored the coast of South America and Balboa crossed the land of Panama and first gazed on another great sea, the Pacific Ocean, to the west.

Voyages of Discovery

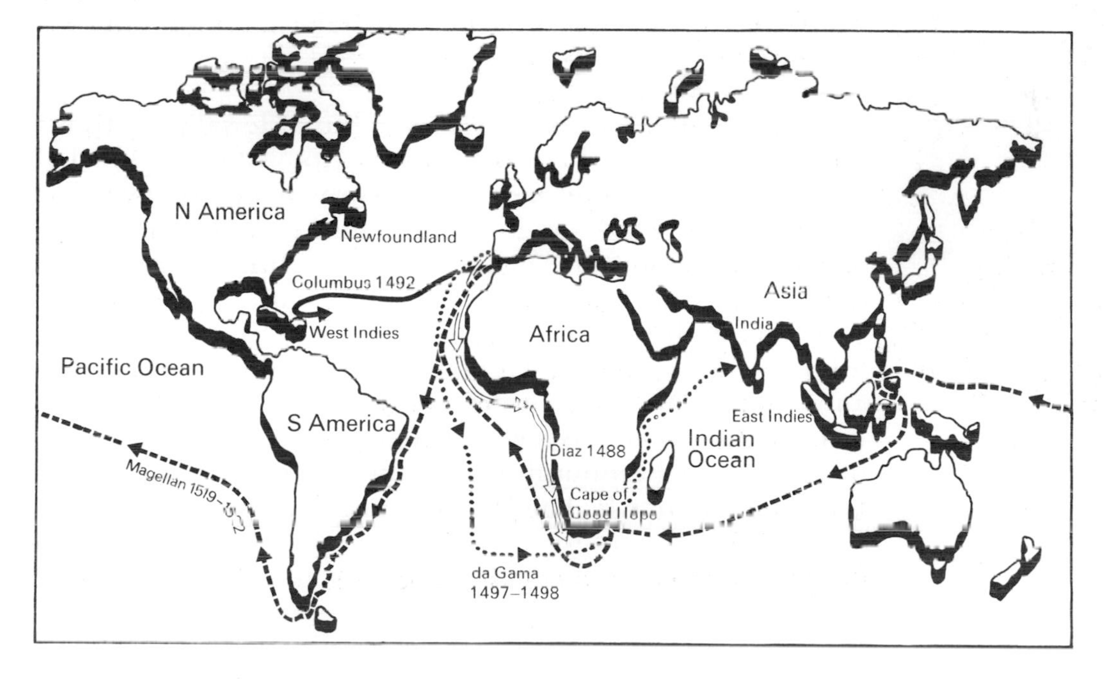

But they had not reached India by sailing west.

In 1519 Ferdinand Magellan set off from Spain with five ships to try to solve the problem. Trying to sail round South America, they made their way through the strait which is now named after him, and entered the Pacific Ocean. They sailed for months, running out of food with never a sight of land. Then they reached the Philippines where Magellan died fighting the natives. His men sailed on, to the East Indies, where they loaded up with food and spices. Then they crossed the Indian Ocean and went on round the Cape of Good Hope, until just one leaking ship and eighteen men got back to Spain. They had sailed right round the world.

They were exciting times, as exciting as our own. Adventurers returned with gold and silver, black men and strange stories. They had conquered the oceans as we have conquered the air and space. A new continent, America, had appeared over the western seas, and the countries facing the Atlantic (Spain, Portugal, France and England) were well placed to become wealthy by trade.

James IV

Scotland under James IV *(1488–1513)*

Let us consider Scotland's position in this new age. The country produced no outstanding artists, scientists or explorers. It stood on the fringe of the great changes in Europe. At the court, however, the king was determined that his country should not be out-of-date. James IV was a great all-rounder, a good athlete and horseman, a keen scientist and surgeon and it was said that he knew Latin and Gaelic and five foreign languages.

He made sure that people obeyed him. He sailed with his fleet to the Western Isles and broke the power of the Lord of the Isles. Then he set more sheriffs over the Highlanders. Keen to know what was going on in his kingdom, James was always on the move. He made tours to see things for himself, and to make sure that justice was being done.

Scotland already had two universities, St Andrews and Glasgow, and James IV founded the third at Aberdeen in 1495, to produce lawyers and, for the first time in Britain, to train doctors as well. A few years later, he recognised the craft of surgery in Edinburgh and allowed no one to carry out operations unless he had been properly trained. In 1496 he ordered barons and freeholders to send their eldest sons to grammar schools at the age of eight or nine, until they had 'perfect Latin and understanding of the laws'. Here, for the first time, was education for boys who were not going to be churchmen.

The printing of books began in 1508, much later than in other countries. In their shop in Edinburgh, Walter Chapman and Andrew Millar published their first volume. It included poems by William Dunbar, who wrote *The Thistle and the Rose* to celebrate the wedding of James to Margaret Tudor of England. Dunbar, a wandering scholar who became one of the king's clerks, was a great poet. He wrote,

The Taill of the Cok, and the Iasp.

Ane cok sũ tyme with feddrã fresch & gay,
Richt cãt & crous albeit he was bot pure
Flew furth vpõ ane dunghill sone be day
To get his dennar set was al his cure.
Scraipand amang the as be auenture,
He fand ane Iolie Iasp, richt precious,
Wes castin furth in sweping of the hous.

As Damisellis wantoun, and Insolent,
That fane wald play, and on the streit be sene,
To swoping of the hous thay tak na tent.

Thay

An example of early printing (1571). Henryson's fable about the cock who found a 'jasp' or precious jewel in a midden not in Latin, but in the language of his own people. Gavin Douglas translated the works of Latin poets like Virgil and Horace into 'the braid Scots'. A Dunfermline schoolmaster, Robert Henryson, told fascinating stories about animals in his *Moral Fables*. What do you think of his description of the worried little mouse in these lines?

> Ane lytill mous come till ane rever [river] syde;
> Scho [she] micht not waid, hir schankis [legs] were sa short,
> Scho culd not swym, scho had na hors to ryde;
> Of verray force behovit [of necessity forced] her to byde,
> And to and fra besyde the Rever deip
> Scho ran, cryand with mony pietuous [pitiful] peip.

James IV was curious about science and bought books and chemicals, and carried out experiments on his own. He was taken in by John Damian, a foreigner, and spent a lot of money on him. Damian claimed that he could turn other metals into gold, and even tried to become the first man to fly. Wearing wings made of feathers, he leapt from the walls of Stirling Castle, but with no success,

> And in the myre [mud], up till the een [eyes],
> Among the glaur did glyde,

according to Dunbar, who made fun of Damian's efforts.

When English pirates interfered with Scottish trading vessels in the Firth of Forth, Sir Andrew Wood of Largo in Fife went out with two ships, the *Flower* and the *Yellow Carvel*, to fight them. After a desperate battle, he captured the five English ships.

To build real fighting ships, James brought ship-builders over from France and the Netherlands. In the royal dockyard at Newhaven near Leith they built stout ships, including the *Great Michael*, the biggest ship of her day. To build her, we are told, men 'cut all the woods of Fife, except Falkland Wood, in addition to all the timber that was brought out of Norway'. Measuring 75 metres from stem to stern, she was armed with more than 300 guns and it took 300 men to sail her. She made Scotland a power to be reckoned with at sea.

The Battle of Flodden

While English troops were fighting against the French in 1513, James declared war on Henry VIII of England. Men from all over Scotland joined him and he advanced over the Border. His big guns won him Wark and Norham castles.

Then he took up such a strong position on Flodden Hill that the Earl of Surrey, the English commander, dared not attack him. But Surrey led his men round the side of the Scottish army and placed them between the Scots and their road back to Scotland. Under cover of smoke the Scots turned to face them. The English artillery out-gunned the Scots, and its accurate fire tore great gaps in the Scottish ranks. The battle was fought on foot, but the Scots, armed with four-and-a-half-metre pikes, lost formation as they crossed the rough ground. These awkward weapons were useless at close quarters against the English halberds or bills, which were much shorter and could be used both as spears and battle-axes. James, who led the charge himself, had his pike shattered, and was killed only a pike's length from the Earl of Surrey. In the hand-to-hand battle that followed, the Scots could not reach the English bill-men with their swords. The Scots 'could not resist the bills that lighted so thick and so sore upon them', and thousands were killed.

It was more a massacre than a battle. Though the Scots had as many men and had more guns and food-supplies, they were a feudal host compared with this English army of professional soldiers, disciplined and armed with a weapon to which the Scots had no answer. Scotland was not as modern as she had thought.

Hand-to-hand fighting at Flodden. Notice how the English bill is a much handier weapon

Something for You to Do

1. For a frieze with the heading *They Began the Modern Age*, work in groups on: *a*) scientists; *b*) printers; *c*) artists; *d*) explorers.
2. *a*) Explain how each of these changed men's lives: gunpowder; the compass; printing; the telescope; America.
   b) Which event would you choose as the beginning of the modern age, and why?
3. Make a map of the voyages of discovery, using a different colour or sign for each explorer's route. For more about them, see *Voyages of Discovery* in Oliver & Boyd's *Exploring History* series.
4. Write down three ways in which James IV encouraged learning in Scotland.
5. *a*) Explain why the Scots were so heavily defeated at Flodden.
   b) Read Jean Elliot's version of *The Flowers of the Forest*.

20 Changes in Religion

1. Scotland, England and Europe

In most towns you will find at least two places of worship, one Church of Scotland and one Roman Catholic, because nowadays not all Christians agree on what they believe or how they should worship. They are free to choose the church they want to attend. Until the sixteenth century, however, everyone in western Europe was a member of the same church, the Roman Catholic Church, under the Pope in Rome. Every town and parish had its church and everybody went to it. Why and how, then, did people split up and become members of different Churches?

The State of the Church in Scotland

Over the years, kings and nobles had given a lot of land to the Church and by the mid-sixteenth century the Church's income had risen to £400 000 a year. A king might compare this with his own income. He had never had more than £45 000 a year. It was no surprise that the king, and the nobles too, wanted to get some of the Church's great wealth for themselves. James IV, for example, made his own son Archbishop of Saint Andrews when he was only eleven years old, so that he could have the income which came from this high position. Nobles asked the king to make them the guardians of abbeys and cathedrals, not because they wanted to protect them, but to share in the money that flowed into them. Men like these did not help the Church to do its work.

When abbeys became rich, some men wanted to be monks because it had become a comfortable life. In 1534, for example, it was found that every monk in Melrose Abbey had a private garden and was receiving money of his own to spend on clothes—a far cry from the vow of poverty they must have taken.

By 1560 nearly all the parish churches in Scotland had been taken over by some abbey or cathedral (page 69). These great churches collected the *tithes*, the tenth part the people gave each year from their crops and young animals, and they spent them somewhere else. They sent *vicars* to take the place of the priests, but these men were paid so little that they would not do anything for people until they were paid. This happened, for example, when someone in a family died, as Sir David Lindsay tells us:

> Our vicar took the best cow by the head
> Within an hour, when my father was deid.
> And when the vicar heard tell how that my mother
> Was deid, frae hand he took frae me another

The usual church service was in Latin. The vicars could recite it but many of them did not understand it. The Archbishop of St Andrews tried to improve things by issuing to the clergy a new book in Scots to instruct the people. He ordered them to practise reading it so that they would not stammer when they read in church and be laughed at by the congregation. He also told bishops and priests to preach at least four times a year.

Printing, too, played its part. William Tyndale's translation of the Bible into English was published, and traders brought copies back with them to Scotland. When people, and especially scholars, studied the Gospel they found fault with some things that the priests were teaching.

Martin Luther

The Reformation in Europe

Martin Luther, a German professor, was the first to raise his voice in anger. Hearing that a friar was selling 'pardons' for sins, even for the sins of relatives long dead, he could not keep quiet. He felt that a man would be forgiven if he were truly sorry for his sin. Here he saw his countrymen paying for what he thought were worthless promises. Hard-earned German money was going to Rome to help to build the magnificent Church of St Peter. He made a list of ninety-five arguments against these pardons, and nailed them to the church door in Wittenberg in 1517.

Luther began to attack other faults in the Church and the Pope himself. The Pope drove him out of the Church, and the Emperor made him an outlaw. Luther burned the Pope's letter in the market place, but he then had to go into hiding. He translated the Bible into German. The hymn he wrote, *A Safe Stronghold our God is Still*, had half Germany singing. A law was passed which would have crushed the churches which Luther's followers were setting up. Many of the German princes protested, and were given the name *Protestants*.

Luther had tried to point out a fault in the Church, but the Pope would not correct it. The movement Luther started, called the *Reformation*, split the Church and divided people into Catholics and Protestants.

After this the Catholic Church began to put its own house in order. Its chief reformer was a Spanish soldier, Ignatius Loyola. After being severely wounded in battle, he decided to become a soldier for Christ. He formed a new order, the Society of Jesus, whose members were called Jesuits. They started fine schools, and trained priests who went into every land to give the Catholic answers to the new ideas.

Scotland and England

Patrick Hamilton was one of the Scottish students who had attended universities in Europe and came back filled with Luther's ideas. For what he preached he was burned at the stake in St Andrews. Burning him however, did not make people forget him, and it was said, 'the reek of master Patrick Hamilton infected as many as it blew upon'.

Scotland's king, James V, married a Frenchwoman, Mary of Guise in 1538. This bound him to support both the Auld Alliance with France, and the Church of Rome. In England, on the other hand, King Henry VIII, wishing to rid himself of his wife, quarrelled with the Pope. He got Parliament to make him head of the Church in England. He closed all the abbeys, drove out the monks and took their lands. To stop Scotland helping France, Henry's army came north and routed the Scots at *Solway Moss* in 1542. James died heart-broken, leaving a new-born girl to become the beautiful but unfortunate Mary, Queen of Scots.

Henry suggested that his son, Edward, and the child, Mary, should marry when they were old enough. This would have broken off Scotland's alliance with France and united Scotland and England. When the Scots refused, Henry sent his army north under the Earl of Hertford. They captured Edinburgh and set it on fire; it burned for four days. They boasted that in all they burned or cast down 192 towns, towers, churches and farmsteads and drove off 10 000 cattle, 12000 sheep and 1000 horses over the Border. The next year, 1545, Hertford was back, burning the grain harvest and the Border abbeys as well. He returned two years later and smashed another Scottish army at *Pinkie*, near Musselburgh.

These raids, called the 'Rough Wooing' did not win the hearts of the Scots. Instead, Mary was sent to France to be

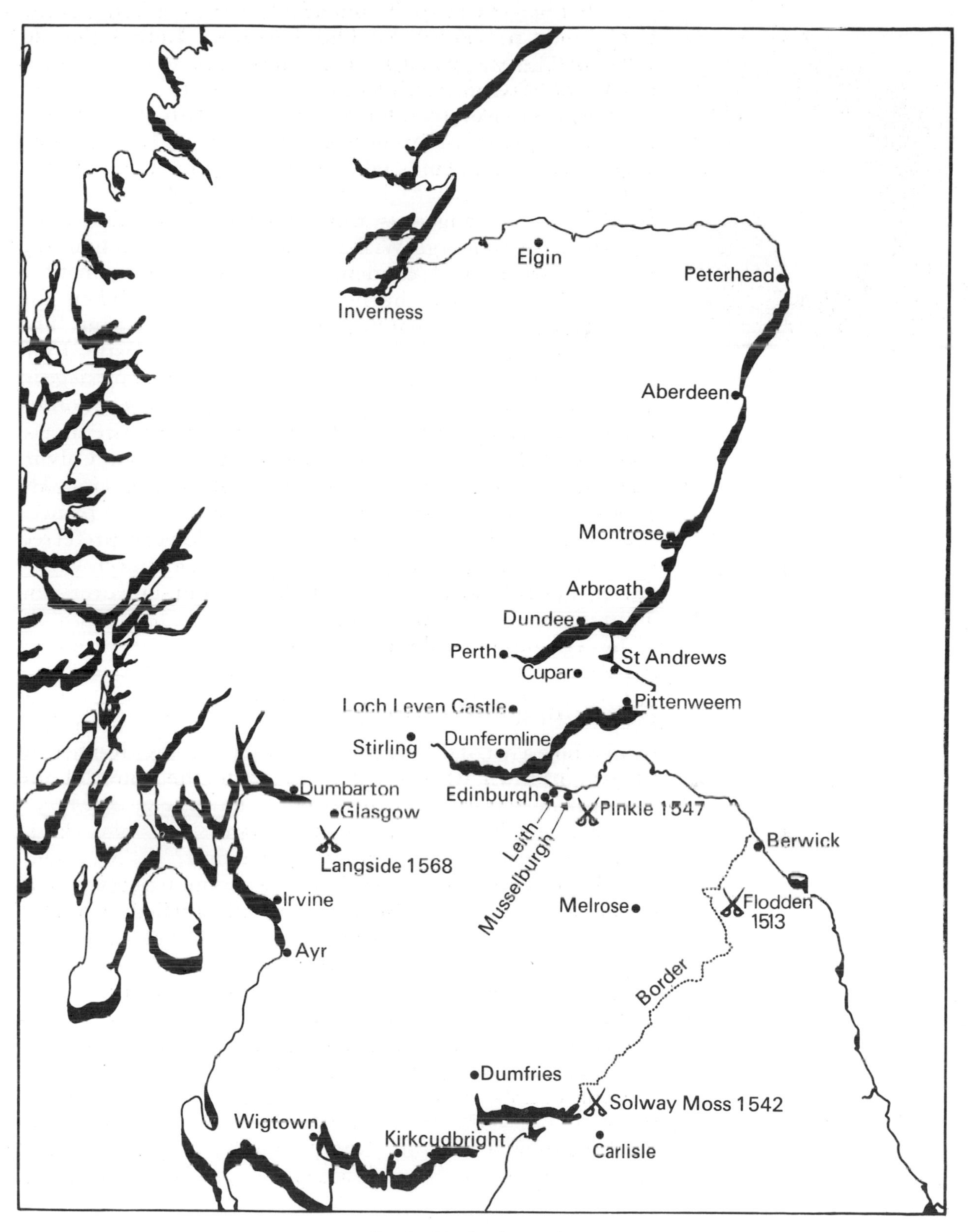

Scotland in the sixteenth century

George Wishart

brought up in safety. But it did help to destroy the old Church. This was the time when people learned more about the Word of God as Bibles in English were brought into seaports and over the Border. The Scottish nobles were interested to learn how people like them in England had become rich when lands taken from the abbeys passed into their hands.

These were dangerous times, however, for Protestant preachers, but George Wishart was one who still took the risk. He was arrested, condemned for preaching against the Catholic Church and burned in St Andrews. Then the Catholic leader, Cardinal Beaton, was killed in revenge. The men who killed him held out in St Andrews Castle. John Knox joined them but they were captured after a long siege in 1547 and sent to France as prisoners. After nineteen months rowing as a galley-slave, John Knox became a minister in the free city of Geneva. He came under the spell of John Calvin, the French Protestant minister who ruled the city. He learned to put his faith in the people rather than in princes and bishops. He saw that Calvin's followers preferred sermons to ceremonies, and worshipped in a church which was plain and undecorated. Back in Scotland, however, few Protestants were still preaching.

In 1559 John Knox came back to Scotland.

Something for You to Do

1. *a*) Make a list of the exact names of some of the churches in your town. Beside each one write the name of the greater church to which each belongs, e.g. St Mary's Parish Church – Church of Scotland.
   b) How many different kinds did you find?
2. Why were *a*) King James IV, *b*) the common people and *c*) the Archbishop of St Andrews dissatisfied with the Church before the Reformation?
3. Under the heading *They Made Changes in Religion*, write short notes on Martin Luther, Ignatius Loyola, John Calvin.
4. What is the meaning of: tithe, Protestant, Jesuit, the 'Rough Wooing'?

21 Changes in Religion

2. *Ministers, Monarchs and Nobles*

In 1558 Mary, Queen of Scots married Francis, the heir to the French throne. In Scotland her mother, Mary of Guise, ruling for her as queen regent, ordered that no one was to preach the Protestant faith. John Knox preached: it was an act of rebellion. This looming figure with the long face, the commanding eyes and flowing black beard thundered against the Church of Rome. People who heard him in Perth were roused by his message and began to smash the stained-glass windows and images in the town's churches. He raised his voice to stop them but he could not control them. Dundee and Ayr were two other places where Protestant ideas took hold.

The regent sent for more troops from France, where her daughter Mary had become queen. Knox's main support came from the lords. They asked for help from England, now Protestant under Queen Elizabeth. She answered by sending an English fleet to the Firth of Forth and 9000 men over the Border. Here was a change of policy indeed! English troops were in Scotland to help the Scots. The French defended the port of Leith with great skill, but in 1560 the regent died and the garrison had to surrender.

1560 was an important year. The *Treaty of Edinburgh* forced the French and English troops to leave Scotland. The Auld Alliance was at an end. No longer would the Scots and French fight together against the English. The Auld Alliance had led to much fighting on the Border, and sent many Scots to die on fields like Flodden. It had kept Scotland in close touch with centres of learning in Europe. Churchmen travelled to and fro, and Scottish students went to study at the University of Paris. French words found their way into Scots—words like *fash, ashet* and *gardyloo.* But as Scotland became Protestant she found that she had more in common with Protestant England than with Catholic France.

John Knox

John Knox became minister of St Giles' in Edinburgh. Parliament met and asked the ministers to agree on what they

John Knox

believed. This statement, called *The Confession of Faith*, owed much to the writings of John Calvin. The ministers relied on the Bible and saw that explaining it, 'the preaching of the Word', was their main duty. The Pope's power in Scotland was to end, and Mass was not to be celebrated.

How was the new Church to be run? Knox provided his answer in *The First Book of Discipline*. He said members of each parish church were to choose their own minister. They were also to elect elders from their members every year to help to run their church. All the churches in each region were to be supervised by a senior minister called a *superintendent*. The affairs of the Church as a whole were to be discussed every year at a great meeting of ministers and laymen from all over Scotland. This parliament of the Church still meets, and is called the *General Assembly*.

With these ideas the nobles in Parliament agreed, but they could not consent to the wealth of the old Church being taken over by the new one. In fact, many of the church lands were already in the hands of the very lords who were sitting in this

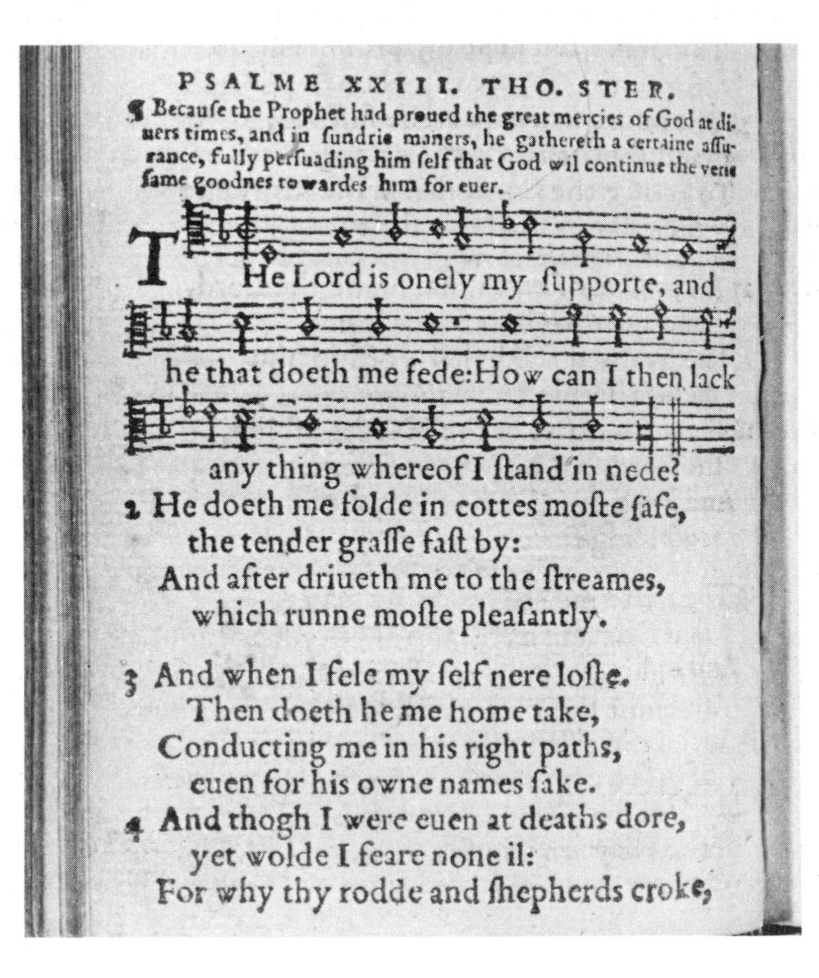

PSALME XXIII. THO. STER.

¶ Becauſe the Prophet had proued the great mercies of God at diuers times, and in ſundrie maners, he gathereth a certaine aſſurance, fully perſuading him ſelf that God wil continue the verie ſame goodnes towardes him for euer.

THe Lord is onely my ſupporte, and he that doeth me fede: How can I then lack any thing whereof I ſtand in nede?

2 He doeth me folde in cottes moſte ſafe,
the tender graſſe faſt by:
And after driueth me to the ſtreames,
which runne moſte pleaſantly.

3 And when I fele my ſelf nere loſte,
Then doeth he me home take,
Conducting me in his right paths,
euen for his owne names ſake.

4 And thogh I were euen at deaths dore,
yet wolde I feare none il:
For why thy rodde and ſhepherds croke,

Psalm 23 as printed in Edinburgh in 1565

Parliament. Because there was no money the bold scheme John Knox had to set up a school in every parish and a college in every town, leading on to the three universities, could not be put into practice. Scotland missed a great chance to provide schools for children all over the country.

Saints' days were no longer to be observed as holidays. To people who used to like them as times to enjoy themselves, the Reformation seemed to have a solemn face.

Mary Queen of Scots

Mary, Queen of Scots

On a misty morning in 1561 Mary, Queen of Scots landed on Scottish soil. She had succeeded to the throne as an infant, but before she was six had been sent for safety to France, her mother's country. She was happy there, and in 1559 her husband, Francis, became King of France. Francis fell ill and died and Mary, a widow at eighteen, resolved to return to Scotland. She was a Catholic, and Scotland had just declared itself Protestant. On her first Sunday in Holyrood Palace she went to Mass as usual and John Knox declared that this was 'more fearful to him than if ten thousand armed enemies were landed in any part of the realm' [kingdom].

Everything she did was criticised. Dancing and laughter in Holyrood Palace one evening were sure to be condemned by John Knox in the pulpit of St Giles the next day. This well-educated, high-spirited, almost foreign queen was sure to need all her courage and charm to deal with scheming lords and the people in Edinburgh set against her by John Knox.

In religion she remained a faithful Catholic, but undertook to maintain the Protestant Church in Scotland. This may appear to be a strange policy for a Catholic queen, but Mary's advisers realised the power the Protestant lords and ministers had. They knew, too, that Mary Tudor had tried to make the English people Catholic again and had failed. Most important of all, Mary always hoped that she would succeed Elizabeth as queen of England or replace her one day. So she was determined never to do anything to disturb the Protestant Church.

Still the Protestants had reason to fear her. She removed one rival by marrying him. He was Lord Darnley, a Catholic who, after herself, was the next heir to the English throne. Plot and murder followed. Darnley was jealous of David Rizzio, the queen's Italian secretary. He was a party to the plot when Rizzio was murdered in Holyrood before the queen's eyes.

In 1567, Darnley lay in Kirk o' Field near Edinburgh, so marked with sores that he wore a mask to hide his face. There was an explosion, and 'the hous was raisett up from the ground with pouder'. Darnley was dead. It was discovered that he had been strangled before the explosion. The Earl of Bothwell, the most powerful man in Scotland, was blamed, but he had so many armed men in Edinburgh that his trial was a farce. The queen, who had been nursing Darnley had gone back to Holyrood that evening to attend an entertainment. Had she known about the plot? We do not know, but three months later she married Bothwell.

The Protestant lords turned against them. Mary was imprisoned on an island in Loch Leven, where she was forced to give up the throne, while Bothwell left Scotland to become a pirate.

In 1568, Mary escaped with the help of a boy, young Willie Douglas, who stole the keys of the castle and rowed her to the shore. She gathered some support, but her forces were defeated at *Langside* near Glasgow. There was no hope for her in Scotland now. She took the risk and fled to England to throw herself on the mercy of her cousin and rival, Queen Elizabeth. She was kept in one prison or another for nearly twenty years, as English Catholics plotted to take Elizabeth's life and make Mary queen of England in her place. But it was not to be. She was tried at last for knowing about another plot, condemned to death and, as she said, 'delivered from all her cares'.

Andrew Melville and James VI

Many people in Scotland carried on worshipping as Catholics but the Protestant Church seemed secure. Knox was preaching with his usual fire. Even when he was so ill that he had to be helped into the pulpit, 'he was so active and vigorous that he was like to ding that pulpit in blads [break it to pieces] and fly out of it'. Mary's son, the new king, James VI, was only a child, but he would be brought up as a Protestant child, educated by the great Protestant scholar, George Buchanan.

But what kind of Protestant church Scotland would have had not been settled. It could be like the Church of England, which had bishops and the queen as supreme governor.

Or it could be the kind of Kirk of Scotland that Andrew Melville wanted to see. After the death of John Knox, this fine scholar spoke for the Kirk. He believed this was not a

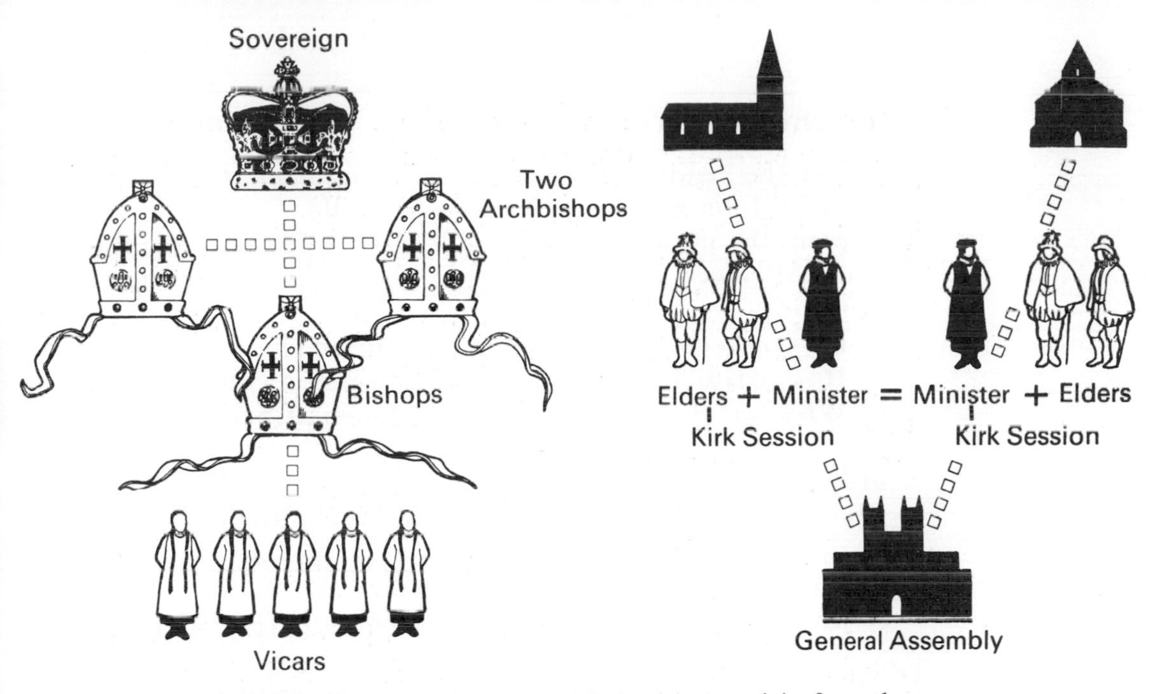

Organisation of the Church of England on the left and the Church of Scotland on the right

matter for the king to settle. He told the king to his face that there were two kingdoms in Scotland—one the king's where he was master, the other Christ's 'whase subject King James the Saxt is, and of whase kingdome [is] nocht a king nor a lord, nor a heid but a member.' Merchants and craftsmen in the towns gave their support. Melville got his way in 1592, when the Presbyterian Kirk was recognised as the Church of Scotland, with complete control over its own affairs. Believing that ministers should be equal, he was against anybody being a superintendent (page 104), which reminded him of a medieval bishop. Instead each Kirk was to have its *session* of elders elected for life, and each district its *presbytery*. Some of the ministers and elders were to meet each year in the General Assembly.

James was not yet defeated. This shambling, parentless boy had struggled to become a man. He learned to trust himself and to fear all men. He gave church lands to many of the nobles and they stopped supporting Melville. James tried to win back control of the Church by appointing bishops. But although the bishops might sit in Parliament they had no power in the Church.

John Knox had brought the Scots into the Protestant faith; he and Andrew Melville decided how the new Church would be organised. But not everyone wanted to worship in the same way, and later kings feared this Church when they had no power over it. Two struggles, one for freedom of worship and the other for control of the Church, were to be fought out in the next century.

Something for You to Do

1. Under the heading *They Made Scotland Protestant*, write notes on John Knox and Andrew Melville.
2. Explain the importance of: the Treaty of Edinburgh; the Auld Alliance; *The First Book of Discipline*; the Battle of Langside.
3. *a*) Do you recognise the psalm on page 104?
   b) If so, write down four lines of the version you know.
4. *a*) Why was it difficult for Mary, Queen of Scots, to rule Scotland?
   b) Why did Queen Elizabeth fear her?
5. Choose a local Presbyterian church. Write down:
   a) the name of the minister;
   b) the names of as many elders as you can;
   c) find out the name of this year's *Moderator* [President] of the General Assembly.
6. The life of Mary, Queen of Scots, has attracted many authors. In *The Escape of the Queen*, Jane Lane describes her escape from Loch Leven Castle. An attempt to rescue Mary is the subject of *A Traveller in Time* by Alison Uttley.

Burntisland Church, built after the Reformation, is square and its tower is in the middle and not at one end like Dalmeny on page 52

22 People in the Sixteenth Century

The Look of the Land

To modern eyes, sixteenth-century Scotland would seem a very poor country. But this was a time when towns were growing and country lairds were building themselves great towers to live in; and writers living then found many things to praise in parts of the country and in some towns. In the Lothians, for example, the villages were bigger with fertile fields around them. Clydesdale with coal-mines as well as good farming land, was described as 'the paradise of Scotland'. Fife, which also had good soil, had coal and salt works and busy little seaports, and was said to be like 'a grey cloth mantle [cloak] with a golden fringe.'

Edinburgh, Dundee and Aberdeen were the biggest towns, and Perth and Montrose other busy trading places. Edinburgh, the capital, was praised for having a High Street which was as wide as a market place. Glasgow was an open town round the cathedral then and a visitor wrote of it, 'This flourishing city reminds me of the beautiful fabrics [cloths or buildings] and the florid [full of flowers] fields of England.'

Smailholm Tower in Roxburghshire, built in the early sixteenth century

Country People

Let us consider the people who lived in Scotland four hundred years ago. Most of them have left no records, and we know little about them. Country folk lived in the same way as their forefathers had done, keeping flocks, cultivating the infield and keeping off the marshy low land. In normal years, they produced enough to keep themselves alive. They had plenty of sheep and cattle, and fish were abundant, but because of their primitive farming methods and wet summers, grain harvests were sometimes poor. In years of famine, for example, 1594–8, some people starved: in years of plenty, some corn was exported.

The Highlanders lived mainly on meat, milk and cheese from their herds, and fish from the rivers. In the Lowlands bread was more common. Oatmeal made the porridge, the brose, the bannocks and the oatcakes eaten by most of the people. Pease-meal, a flour made from ground pease, was the food of the poorest.

When men were not working hard in the fields, they would be cutting wood or peat for the fire. Women were always busy, grinding corn, baking on the girdle or making the family clothes.

Border Reivers

In the Borders, riding into the north of England and stealing cattle was so common that it might almost be called an industry. The men who did it were called 'Border Reivers.' Walter Scott of Harden, 'Auld Wat' as he was called, was the most famous of them. When stocks of meat were running low his wife, Mary, would lay before him at dinner-time an ashet [a serving dish] with nothing on it but a pair of spurs. This was the sign for him to lead his men over the Cheviots again. Will H. Ogilvie describes their ride in his poem, *Ho! For the Blades of Harden*:

> The dark has heard them gather,
>   The dawn has bowed them by,
> To the guard on the roof comes the drum of a hoof
>   And the drone of a hoof's reply.
> There are more than birds on the hill to-night,
>   And more than winds on the plain!
> The threat of the Scotts has filled the moss,
>   'There will be moonlight again'.

Of course, the English also crossed the Border to steal cattle, as you may read in the ballad, *Jamie Telfer of the Fair Dodhead.*

The Parson of Stobo

Before the Reformation, clergymen did not always wear dark clothes, as we learn when we meet Adam Colquhoun. He is the parson of Stobo in Peebleshire but he lives near Glasgow Cathedral. He draws an income of two thousand pounds Scots a year from two parishes in the upper Tweed Valley, which he visits sometimes to supervise the vicar whom he pays to take his place.

As he stands at the manse door to greet us, we are struck by the brightness of his clothes: the scarlet of his doublet [jacket] and waistcoat, the whiteness of his shirt, the gold trimmings on his belt and his velvet cap. Over his arm he carries a fine gown with a fur collar. He likes velvet, the dearest of cloths, and marten, the choicest of furs.

His house is a great stone tower. It is dark as we stumble up the spiral staircase. In the hall, we admire the fine tapestries which cover the stone walls. Then we gaze at the fire, a fire of 'black stones' [coal] burning in an iron grate. In this room the parson eats at his meat-board, a table-top resting on trestles. He opens his carved cupboard to show us his treasures: forty silver plates and vessels, two dozen silver spoons, a dozen small knives and a fork. To have all these knives and a fork is very uncommon, because men usually carry their own knives with them or use their daggers for cutting meat, and lift food with their fingers instead of using forks.

What the Parson of Stobo's hall might have been like

He is well off for what he calls 'belly cheer'. In his barn he has wheat, barley and oats, and in his cellar eight salted carcasses of beef, eight dozen salmon, six stones [about 38 kilograms] of butter, plenty of cheeses, oatmeal and herring.

He is proud of his bedroom. He sleeps in a fine, carved bed, on a soft feather mattress, with fine sheets, two plaids and two blankets to keep him warm. Curtains hang round the bed to keep out the draught. There is so much to amaze the ordinary man of Colquhoun's time: a bed which is a piece of furniture, walls whose stonework is hidden behind the tapestry hangings, the oak settle by the fireplace, the wardrobe for keeping clothes in and his chests full of valuables. Suddenly there is a squawk and we shriek in terror. It's a bird, a bird of many colours with a hooked beak! The parson talks to it and tells us that it is his pet, a parrot.

Later, a change in dress took place. In 1575, ministers and their wives were ordered not to wear bright colours, embroidered clothes or jewellery. All their clothes were to be of dark colours, such as 'black, russet, sad grey, sad brown'. From this law 'clerical grey', the colour we usually expect ministers to wear, was born.

Merchants

Until 1560, Scotland and England were enemies and not much trade took place between them. It was across the North Sea, especially to the Netherlands, that Scottish merchants shipped their goods. To the Flemish weavers went raw wool from the ports of Leith, Aberdeen and Dundee. This was by far the most valuable export and the king made money out of it, too, because his officers collected one pound in customs duty after 1360 on every sack of wool. The ports of the north-east sent out salted salmon while Pittenweem, Leith, Dumbarton, Ayr and Irvine exported herrings. Almost everything Scottish merchants sold abroad came from either farming or fishing.

One Scottish merchant, Andrew Halliburton, kept a detailed account of everything he bought and sold. Bishops, dukes and merchants were customers of his. He states in a letter in 1502 that he sold one sack of wool for twenty-two merks [nearly three pounds], and another sack for twenty-three merks, and adds, 'Hides, I think, shall be the best merchandise [things to sell] to come here at Easter for there are many folk that ask about them'. He brought back a mixture of goods in his ship: lengths of coloured cloth, books, hats, floor-tiles, wine, spices, thread for embroidery, church vessels and a tombstone.

We may say generally that Scotland gave large quantities of a few simple products in return for smaller amounts of a wide range of luxury goods.

Scottish merchants who traded abroad were ordered to be well dressed, so that foreigners would think well of them. They might not all be wealthy but they learned to look their best. Different laws were needed at home. The ordinary man in the burghs could be recognised by his 'blue bonnet and plaid' but it seems some people had been guilty of dressing too well. In 1581 families with land worth less than 2000 merks a year (two-thirds of what Adam Colquhoun had, page 111) were ordered not to wear cloth of gold or silver, velvet or satin or even imported wool.

Francis Spottiswood, is a cloth merchant, who sells downstairs from his house in Edinburgh. He is wearing a brown coat and red stockings, but what catches our eye is his purse. It has gold tassels on it and hangs from his belt. Truly a man of money! He picks a bale of woollen cloth from the nearest chest, and unrolls it on the counter for us to inspect. When he takes us into his house, we see in the hall or main room, a table and cupboard like the parson of Stobo's. Francis Spottiswood has been spending his money on luxuries: a tablecloth, a silver salt-cellar and a chair for himself at the head of the table. Over in the corner is his suit of armour, his

Huntly House, Canongate, Edinburgh, once three houses with gable ends facing the street and upstairs rooms overhanging it. Francis Spottiswoode may have lived in a house like one of these

Carpenters putting up timber framing for the upper rooms of a house like Huntly House about 1600 (a reconstruction by Geoffrey Hay)

helmet and his two-handed sword. He has always to be ready to defend the town.

The bedroom is not only a place to sleep in. Mrs Spottiswood has a 'muckle wheel' in it for spinning. An important invention, the 'muckle wheel' can spin yarn simply by turning the wheel. Mrs Spottiswood tells us how pleased she is that the old, tiring way of spinning with a spindle and whorl is dying out and that many homes now have a 'muckle wheel'. She spins quite quickly but she has to wind the yarn by hand. 'What is that over there?' you say to yourself. You can see yourself in it. Mrs Spottiswood calls it a 'keiking glass'.

Francis Spottiswood, the cloth merchant, also owns a horse and a plough, harrows, a cart and a sledge. Like other burgesses, he has a share in 'the burgh acres', from which most of his food comes.

Schoolboys

Most boys and girls did not go to school at all. As soon as they were old enough they helped in the fields or in the house. In the burghs, boys became apprentices and learned a trade. For boys at school, the hours were long. At Aberdeen Grammar School, scholars had already spent two hours in class by nine o'clock in the morning. After an hour's break, they were back at their lessons until twelve o'clock, and in the afternoon they were at work from two until four and again from five o'clock until six. The main subject in grammar schools was Latin but James Melville, who went to school in Montrose, says they also studied the Bible and French, and 'be our maister war teached to handle the bow for archerie, the glub for goff, the batons for fencing, also to rin, to loope, to swoom, to warsell'.

Something for You to Do

1. The population of Scotland is more than five times greater than it was in 1557, but some places have grown far more than others. Here are the chief Scottish burghs in order of importance in 1557 and 1974.

1557 *(Based on taxable value)*	1974 *(Based on population)*
Edinburgh	Glasgow
Dundee	Edinburgh
Aberdeen	Dundee
Perth	Aberdeen
St Andrews	Paisley
Montrose	Motherwell (and Wishaw)
Cupar	East Kilbride
Ayr	Greenock
Glasgow	Dunfermline
Dunfermline	Coatbridge
Dumfries	Kilmarnock
Inverness	Kirkcaldy
Stirling	Ayr

   a) Is your town here? Has it risen or fallen compared with other burghs in Scotland, and why?
   b) Which have risen most, and why?
2. Explain these to an Englishman: Border Reivers; 'sad grey'; 'belly cheer', 'muckle wheel'; 'keiking glass'.
3. Make a list of the luxuries which the parson and merchant owned but which most people in the sixteenth century did not have.
4. Make a list of the things in a modern council house which make it more comfortable and easier to manage than a laird's tower like Smailholm on page 109.
5. Look at the picture of men building a house on page 114, and describe what each of them is doing.
6. Rewrite in English what James Melville was taught at school.

23 The Struggle for Freedom

1. The Reign of James VI and I

Stewart Rulers of Scotland and England 1603–1714			
James VI and I:	1603-25	James VII and II:	1685–88
Charles I:	1625–49	William and Mary:	1689–1702
(The Commonwealth:	1649–60)	(Mary died–1694)	
Charles II:	1660–85	Anne:	1702–14

The Union of the Crowns

To the lives of most Scottish people the year 1603 brought no change. In 1603, however, Queen Elizabeth, the last of the Tudors, died. She had named James VI of Scotland to succeed her. To James the news was like a dream come true. England was a powerful nation, whose sailors like Sir Francis Drake had faced the Spanish Armada and scattered or sunk its ships only fifteen years before. England was a far richer country, both in crops and trade. England also had a Church after his own heart, a Church with bishops in control. 'Jamie Saxt', King of Scotland, became James I, King of England without a blow struck in anger. Little wonder he felt that God was on his side!

A waxworks statue of James VI about the time he became James I of England

James and his courtiers departed for London, the capital of his greater kingdom. He was not sorry to leave Scotland. For years the nobles had struggled to control him, and the ministers of the Kirk had declared from their pulpits that he had no control over them. He was to come back to Scotland only once in the next twenty-two years. Only the merchants of Edinburgh were sorry to see him go, as many of his nobles went with him and would buy their wines, cloth and other luxuries in London in future.

Although all of Great Britain was now under one king, Scotland and England remained separate in other ways. They kept their own systems of law. Their Churches were different; the Church of England was Episcopalian, that is, governed by bishops, but in Scotland the Kirk was Presbyterian, with kirk sessions and General Assembly. The bishops James had appointed in Scotland sat in Parliament, but at first they had no power in the Kirk. Each country kept its own parliament. James tried to bring the two nations closer together, but the English Parliament did not agree to his proposals.

James in England

James had trouble with the English Parliament from the start. Parliament said that the king could not make laws or tax people if it did not agree. If the king did not recognise its rights it could cut off his supply of money. Parliament was now demanding far more from a foreign king like James than it had dared from Queen Elizabeth.

In James's time, no one thought that all men should be free to worship as they pleased. They could not have imagined that we would have many different churches today, or that people would be able to go to any church they liked. This is called *religious toleration*, but in the seventeenth century, each group believed it was the only one which worshipped in the right way, and each tried to convert all the others to its beliefs and services.

Many English people were *Puritans*. They lived strict lives, they liked to read the Bible and wanted to worship in a simple manner. When James met some of them at Hampton Court in 1604, they had high hopes of him. Coming from Scotland he would surely make some of the changes that they wanted to see in the Church of England. But when they mentioned Presbytery, where, as he said, 'Tom and Will and Dick may meet and censure [find fault with] me', James was furious. They reminded him of the struggles he had had with the Kirk in Scotland. He refused to let them have their own way, but he did agree to a new translation of the Bible being made. This, the *Authorised Version* as it is known, is still used by Protestants today. It is addressed to him, calling him 'the Most High and Mighty Prince, James, by the Grace of God, King of Great Britain, France and Ireland, Defender of the Faith'.

In 1620, some Puritans known as the 'Pilgrim Fathers' set sail from Plymouth in the ship *Mayflower*. They braved the wild Atlantic to seek their freedom in America.

Roman Catholics in England, knowing that his mother had been a Catholic, were also disappointed in him. The plot by some Catholics to blow up James and Parliament with gunpowder was discovered, and Guy Fawkes was arrested in a cellar on 4th November 1605. Nowadays, before the Queen opens Parliament, the Yeoman of the Guard always inspect the cellars. The Fifth of November, when the Houses of Parliament were to have been blown up, is still 'Guy Fawkes Night'.

James and Scotland

Even from London, James was able to rule Scotland easily, through men who would do what he told them. He was sure that the Scottish Parliament would obey him, because 'his men' were certain of being members of a group called the *Committee of the Articles*. It decided which 'articles' or bills pleased the king, and passed them on to Parliament which met simply to agree to them. James spoke the truth when he declared:

> 'This I must say for Scotland and may truly vaunt [boast] it. Here I sit and govern it with my pen. I write and it is done, and by a Clerk of the Council I govern Scotland now, which others could not do by the sword'.

He worked away quietly to try to gain control over the Church of Scotland. The General Assembly had been the place where the ministers and elders made their voices heard, but he would not let it meet. He appointed bishops and gave them real power. These things made him feel he was master over the Kirk. His next step was to bring in the same kind of church service as was used in the Church of England. People were told, for example, to kneel down when they were taking Communion. But it was one thing to make changes: it was far more difficult to make people obey them, as Charles I, James' son, was soon to discover.

Something for You to Do

1. Why was James VI keen to become king of England?
2. Find out more about Queen Elizabeth and some of the men who made England famous in the Elizabethan age.
3. *a*) Why did James favour the Church of England?
   b) How did he deal with (*i*) the Puritans, and (*ii*) the Catholics in England?
4. How was James able to rule Scotland 'with the pen'?
5. Make a time-chart of *Britain in Stewart Times* (1603–1707), using a suitable scale, with columns for *Date*, *Ruler*, *Events in Scotland* and *Events in England*. Put in important events from this and later chapters.

24 The Struggle for Freedom

2. *Charles I and Cromwell*

When Charles I became king in 1625, he was the first king of Scotland to be more an Englishman than a Scot. He ruled from London as his father had done, but he did not know the Scots and did not understand the Church of Scotland. The Scottish Parliament did what he wanted: it was the Kirk he had most to fear.

Soon he made other enemies. Many of the Scottish nobles had lands which had once belonged to the Church. Their families had held them so long that they thought they owned them. But by an act in 1625 it looked as if the new king was trying to take them all back for himself. This proved not to be true, but the damage was done and many of the nobles turned against the king.

Riot when the new prayer book was read in St Giles', 1637

Charles and the Church in Scotland

Charles ordered that a new Scottish prayer book, like the one used in the Church of England, be read in all the churches in Scotland. He did not think of asking the General Assembly what they thought of it. Its first reading in St Giles' in Edinburgh was met by a shower of stools and stones when riots broke out. This was the first sign that the ordinary people would stand up against the king.

In 1638, the National Covenant was drawn up and signed in Greyfriars' Kirk in Edinburgh. Then, all over the southern half of the country, people eagerly put their names to copies. Those who signed were the *Covenanters*. They promised to defend 'the true religion', that is, the practices of the Church of Scotland, and also to defend the king. You may think that it would be impossible for them to carry out both these promises, since the king seemed to be attacking the Church of Scotland. Most people, however, believed that it was William Laud, the Archbishop of Canterbury, who was giving advice and who brought in the new Prayer Book. The time was to come when those who signed the Covenant had to decide which was their greater loyalty—to their king or to their Church. Most of them chose to fight for the Kirk; some, led by the Marquis of Montrose, preferred to do their duty to the king.

This is how the Scots challenged the king. They were about to fight a war for their religion, like the *Thirty Years' War* (1618–48) which was going on in Europe. Many of their leaders were battle-hardened soldiers who had fought in that war. They had been 'soldiers of fortune' in the armies of Gustavus Adolphus, the Protestant king of Sweden. Their leader was the 'old, little, crooked soldier', Alexander Leslie, who had risen to command the Swedish forces in Germany after Gustavus was killed. The Covenanters soon had a strong army of 20 000 men. Most of them were 'stout young plewmen. . . . Had ye lent your eare in the morning, or especialle at even, and heard in the tents the sound of some singing psalms, some praying and some reading scripture, you would have been refreshed.'

When they advanced into England Charles did not have an army strong enough to stop them. He had to make peace and allow them to have their own Kirk again. He had lost control of Scotland completely.

Roundhead

The Covenanters and the Civil War

Early in his reign, Charles had quarrelled with the English Parliament, and for the next eleven years (1629–40) he had been ruling without it. Now, because he needed extra money to pay for an army, he had to call Parliament again. Parliament wanted to cut the power he had and stop him ruling on his own again. The two sides could not agree, and the *Civil War* in England broke out.

Charles's followers, the *Cavaliers*, came from the ranks of the country landowners and their men, while Parliament's army nicknamed *Roundheads*, consisted mainly of craftsmen and merchants from the towns, and prosperous farmers like Oliver Cromwell. Most of the Roundheads were Puritans, and some were Presbyterians like the Scots.

The two sides were evenly matched: the support of the Scottish army could tip the scales. The Covenanters agreed to fight on Parliament's side, if the religion of England was changed 'according to the word of God and the example of the best reformed Churches'. To the Scots, that meant the Presbyterian Church. They had started fighting against the king because he tried to force his religion on them: the Scots were now trying to force a Church like their own on the English people. In 1644, at *Marston Moor* in Yorkshire, the Scottish foot-soldiers helped Oliver Cromwell's magnificent cavalry, the *Ironsides*, to victory over the Cavaliers.

Cavalier. You will see that they did not look so very different from the Roundheads when armed ready for battle

Meanwhile, the Marquis of Montrose, who had signed the National Covenant, decided he could not set aside his oath to defend the king. He raised a small army of Irishmen and Highlanders to fight for King Charles in Scotland, and swept through Scotland like a whirlwind. Thanks to the speed with which he moved his men, their toughness and his own gifts as a leader, he won six victories in a single year between September 1644 and August 1645. Scotland was in his hand. He was ready to invade England to help the king. But the Covenanters under David Leslie surprised his little army at *Philiphaugh* near Selkirk and practically wiped them out.

Successes at Philiphaugh in Scotland and at *Naseby* in England made 1645 a year of victory for Cromwell's army and the Covenanters. Four years later Charles I, a prisoner of the Parliamentary army, was tried by Parliament and put to death on the scaffold. Horror spread among the Scottish people. Many of them had wanted their own religion, but not at the expense of the life of the king. At once they proclaimed his son, Charles II, king of Scotland, but

England became a republic, known as the *Commonwealth*, without a king.

Cromwell and Scotland

Cromwell's army marched north into Scotland. At Dunbar, the Covenanters and the Roundheads, who had been comrades-in-arms at *Marston Moor*, came face to face in battle. The Covenanters were placed in such a strong position by David Leslie that Cromwell did not dare attack them. Then the ministers who were with the army, persuaded him to move his men down the hill. This was just what Cromwell wanted. 'The Lord has delivered them into our hands,' he said, as he sent his Ironsides crashing through the Scottish lines. Another Scottish army invaded England and, exactly a year later on 3rd September 1651, he crushed it at the battle of *Worcester*.

English troops under General Monk kept Scotland quiet. Even in the Highlands, order was kept as it never had been before. As an Englishman observed, 'A man may ride all over Scotland with a switch in his hand and a hundred pounds in his pocket, which he could not have done these five hundred years.' Everyone was given freedom of worship, not that the Church of Scotland wanted this. Scotland also had the right to send members to the new British Parliament in London, but the Scots knew that Scotland and England were held together only by the force of Cromwell's armies.

Something for You to Do

1. Why did *a*) the nobles, *b*) people in the Church turn against Charles I in Scotland?
2. Write notes on: the Scottish Prayer Book; the National Covenant; Cavaliers; Roundheads.
3. Choose *one* of the following: *a*) the Marquis of Montrose; *b*) Alexander Leslie; *c*) David Leslie, and find out more about him.
4. How did Scotland *a*) benefit, and *b*) suffer, under Cromwell?
5. The story of Charles II's escape after the Battle of Worcester is told in Jane Lane's *The Escape of the King*.
6. Continue your time chart.

25 The Struggle for Freedom

3. *From Restoration to Revolution*

When Cromwell died in 1658, there was no strong man to succeed him. General Monk, the commander of the Commonwealth forces in Scotland, was convinced that only the king's return would satisfy the people. He marched his men to London, and recalled Charles II from exile. This ended Britain's only experiment of ruling without a king.

The *Restoration*, as the return of the king was called, took place in 1660. It was an occasion for much rejoicing. The king was back, and Scotland was a separate country once more. But soon the people ceased to rejoice.

Charles II and the Church

Charles controlled Scotland, as his grandfather had done, 'with the pen.' He appointed bishops to rule the Church and declared the National Covenant illegal. He gave the right to choose ministers to local landowners. As a result, two hundred and sixty-two ministers who had not been appointed in this way, mainly in the south-west of Scotland, left their churches. There, and round about Edinburgh, people gathered outside to worship in *conventicles* among the hills.

John Blackadder was a minister who once preached to an assembly of four thousand people near Cramond; John Welsh was the great-grandson of John Knox; Alexander Peden for twenty years lived and preached in the open air, and Richard Cameron held out to the last. Troops were sent to arrest these 'outed' ministers but many people, risking fines and horrible torture, came to hear them. Ministers and people suffered, but they took courage from the word of God: 'Blessed are they which are persecuted for righteousness' sake: for theirs is the kingdom of heaven.'

A Conventicle

See them setting off from the distant village, some walking, some riding, the men carrying weapons, till they reach the

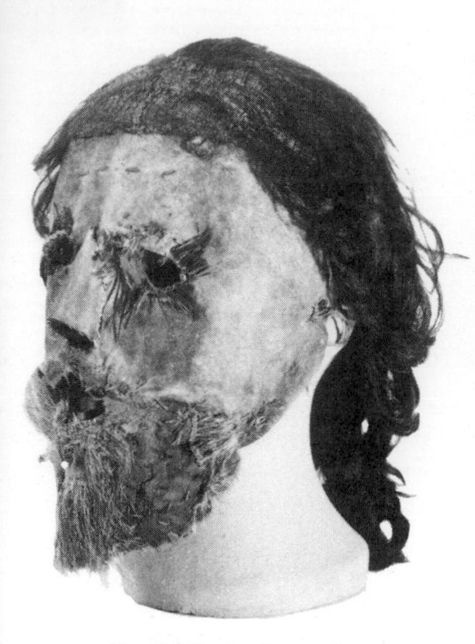
Sandy Peden's mask

appointed hollow in the hills. Sentries are posted to look out in all directions for the hated red-coats. The women pull heather to sit on. 'There now, see that man in black, pulling off his mask. That's the minister, that's Sandy Peden.' He leads them in worship, talking to them in homely, simple terms. 'I will tell you where the Church is,' he says. 'It is wherever a praying young man or young woman is, at a dykeside in Scotland. That is where the Church is.' The service is not interrupted today by the shout of the sentry or the warning cry of the peewit, and when it is over the people return quietly to their homes. The wandering Peden goes to share a meal with them, but will not let them risk being caught giving him shelter at night. Instead he sleeps under the stars.

The Covenanters Fight

People rose up against these laws. They marched in the rain from Galloway and Ayrshire towards Edinburgh, a brave little army, but armed mainly with scythes and pitchforks. In 1666, at *Rullion Green* in the Pentland Hills, royalist forces under Dalyell of the Binns overwhelmed them. Prisoners were tortured and some hanged. This was a 'reign of terror', as soldiers under Dalyell and Graham of Claverhouse scoured the country in search of Covenanters. For a time after this it was made easier for the covenanting ministers to come back into the Church and nearly a hundred did.

Then in 1679, a handful of Covenanters dragged Archbishop Sharp from his coach on Magus Muir near St Andrews and killed him before his daughter's eyes. Sharp had been a Presbyterian minister, but had deserted to the king's side to become a bishop. Both sides gathered troops and a large government army won the battle at *Bothwell Bridge*. A thousand Covenanters were taken prisoner and marched to Edinburgh. Most were pardoned on condition that they would not rebel again, but over two hundred of them were transported to the colonies.

A few extreme rebels held out. They were called *Cameronians* after their leader, Richard Cameron, and were hunted down and put to death. Others were cruelly dealt with. In 1685, for example, Margaret Wilson, a girl of eighteen, and Margaret MacLachlan were tied to stakes on the Solway and drowned by the tide coming in. People like these, who died for what they believed, were *martyrs* and are the subject of Robert Louis Stevenson's famous poem:

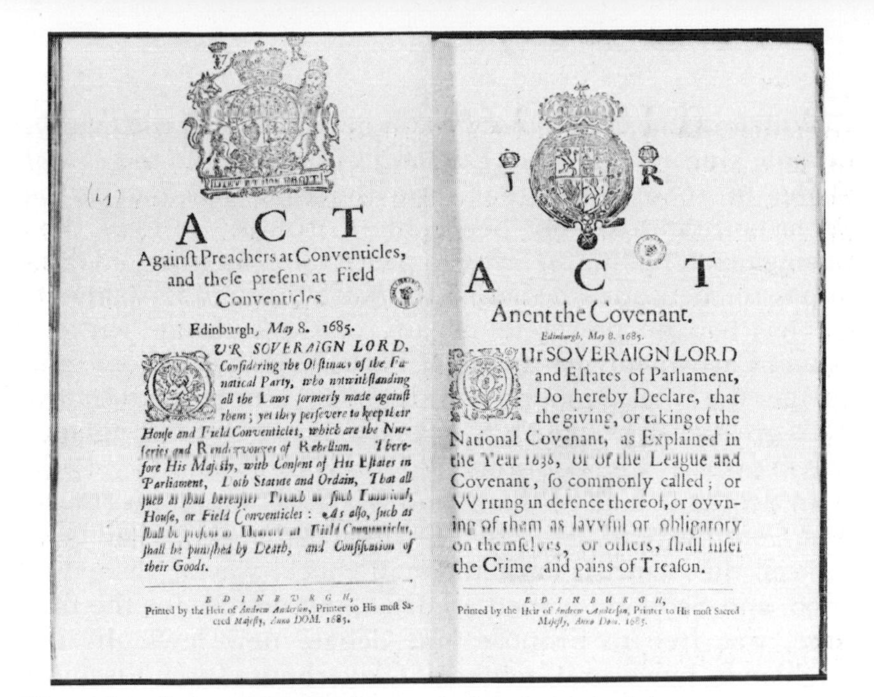

(14)

ACT
Against Preachers at Conventicles, and these present at Field Conventicles

Edinburgh, *May* 8. 1685.

OUR SOVERAIGN LORD, Considering the Obstinacy of the Fanatical Party, who notwithstanding all the Laws formerly made against them; yet they persevere to keep their House and Field Conventicles, which are the Nurseries and Rendezvouses of Rebellion. Therefore His Majesty, with Consent of His Estates in Parliament, Doth Statute and Ordain, That all such as shall hereafter Preach at such Tumultuous, House, or Field Conventicles: As also, such as shall be present as Hearers at Field Conventicles, shall be punished by Death, and Confiscation of their Goods.

EDINBURGH,
Printed by the Heir of *Andrew Anderson*, Printer to His most Sacred *Majesty*, *Anno* DOM. 1685.

J R

ACT
Anent the Covenant.

Edinburgh, May 8. 1685.

OUr SOVERAIGN LORD and Estates of Parliament, Do hereby Declare, that the giving, or taking of the National Covenant, as Explained in the Year 1638, or of the League and Covenant, so commonly called; or VVriting in defence thereof, or ovvning of them as lavvful or obligatory on themselves, or others, shall infer the Crime and pains of Treason.

EDINBURGH,
Printed by the Heir of *Andrew Anderson*, Printer to His most Sacred *Majesty*, *Anno Dom*. 1685.

Acts passed by James VII and Parliament against preachers and people at conventicles and against the Covenants, at the start of his reign in 1685

Blows the wind to-day, and the sun and the rain are flying,
   Blows the wind on the moors to-day and now,
Where about the graves of the martyrs the whaups [curlews] are crying
   My heart remembers how!

Grey recumbent [flat] tombs of the dead in desert places,
   Standing stones on the vacant wine-red moor,
Hills of sheep, and the homes of the silent vanished races,
   And winds austere and pure.

Be it granted me to behold you again in dying,
   Hills of home! And to hear again the call;
Hear about the graves of the martyrs the peewees [lapwings] crying,
   And hear no more at all.

'The Glorious Revolution'

The next king, James VII and II, was a Roman Catholic. In 1687 he issued the first of two *Declarations of Indulgence*, which let Presbyterians and Roman Catholics, as well as members of the Church of England, worship freely. It seemed a sensible way to end so much torture and killing, but perhaps James' main aim was just to help the Roman Catholics. In England, he put Roman Catholics in high positions in the State and in the Army, although this was against the law. When his son was born in 1688, people feared that rule by Catholic kings would go on and on in what was mainly a Protestant country. William of Orange, James's son-in-law, was asked to come over from Holland to save Protestantism in Britain.

William came, and James fled. William, and his wife Mary, became king and queen of England by agreeing to the *Bill of Rights* in 1689. Since that time the ruler has had to be Protestant, and has not been able to rule as he likes. For raising taxes, having an army in peace time, altering old laws or passing new ones, he has had to work through Parliament. He has had no power to do any of these things without asking Parliament. As a result, Parliament has become the partner the king cannot do without in governing the country. This great change, which took place peacefully in England, was known as 'The Glorious, Bloodless Revolution'.

In Scotland, also, William and Mary became joint rulers. The Committee of the Articles, which earlier kings had used to keep the Scottish Parliament in check, was abolished in 1690, and Scotland gained a Parliament which, for the first time, was free to propose and debate new laws. In the Highlands, however, Graham of Claverhouse (now Viscount Dundee) raised the clans for James. He defeated the government troops at the battle of *Killiecrankie* (1689), but when he himself was killed the rebellion came to an end.

Scotland gained the Presbyterian Church most people wanted. The bishops were deposed and the Church was free of royal control. The General Assembly met in 1690, for the first time since the days of Cromwell, and has met every year since. The Kirk had won its struggle against the king. Religious toleration was granted to members of other Protestant Churches, and people began to think that it was right that everyone should be free to worship as he pleased.

Something for You to Do

1. *a*) Why were people pleased to start with when Charles II returned?
   b) Give a reason why they were less pleased later on.
2. Would you call the struggle by the Covenanters a national rebellion, or only a rebellion in some places? Give reasons.
3. Was there a covenanting minister in your district? If so, find out all you can about him and the places where conventicles were held.
4. Why was it a great risk to be a Covenanter and attend conventicles in 1685? (See page 123.)
5. What benefits did the 'Glorious Revolution' bring to Scotland?
6. Continue your time chart.

26 Life in the Highlands in the Seventeenth Century

In the last two hundred years, great numbers of people have left the Highlands. Nowadays every summer sees people with Highland names from southern Scotland, England, the USA and Commonwealth countries like Canada, Australia and New Zealand returning to visit the glens of their ancestors.

Let us take a look at the old way of life of the Highlanders, as it was in the seventeenth century.

The *Highland Line* separated Highlanders who spoke Gaelic from Lowlanders who did not. It runs along the edge of the Highlands where they drop down to the Lowlands, roughly thirty kilometres north of Glasgow, Stirling, Perth and Montrose. It continues northwards and west-

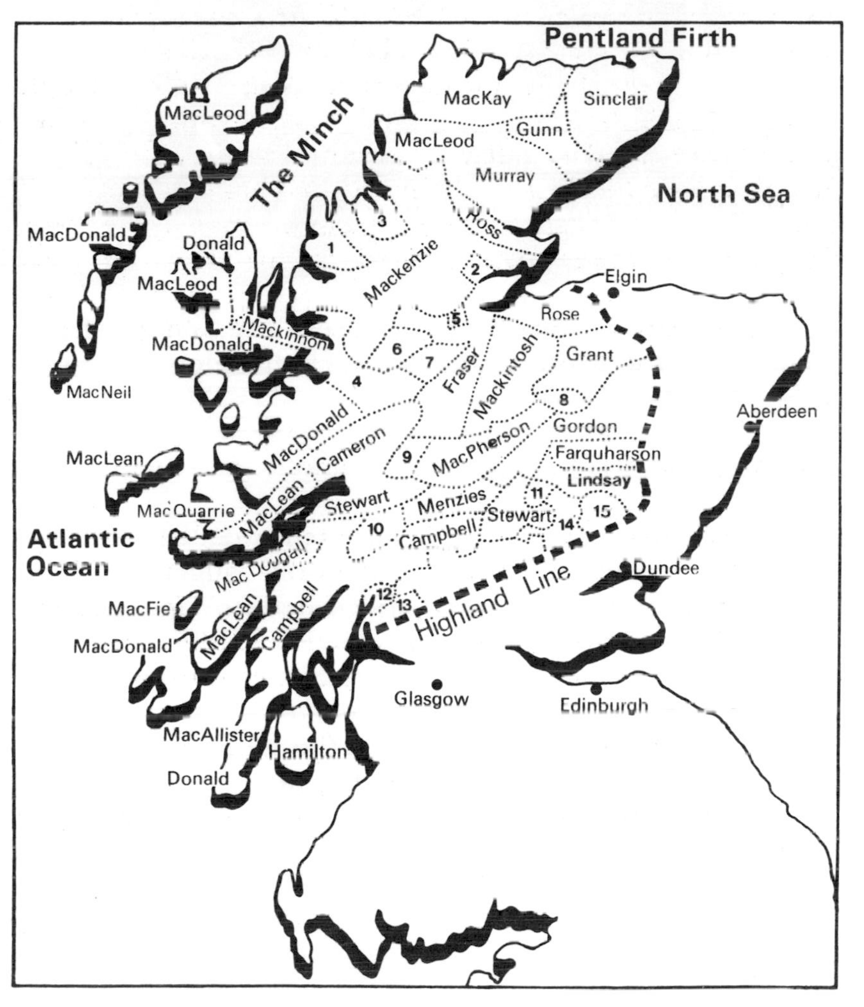

1 MacLeod
2 Munro
3&4 MacDonell of Glengarry
5&6 Chisholm
7 Grant
8 Shaw
9 Ranald MacDonald
10 MacGregor
11 Mackintosh
12 Colquhoun
13 Buchanan
14 Robertson
15 Ogilvy

Clan map of Scotland

A great Highland laird, Sir Duncan Campbell of Glenorchy, with his coat of arms beside him in 1619 when he was 65

wards, leaving out most of Aberdeenshire and the flatter lands along the Moray Firth. The Highlanders live north and west of the Highland Line.

Chiefs and Clans

The Highlanders belonged to clans, each under its own chief. The word *clan*, which means 'the children', suggests that the members of one clan were all related to one another. Certainly, the chief was like an all-powerful father over them. They paid him rents and labour services. He was their judge and his word was law. He was their commander, who could call the clan to war by sending round the 'fiery cross', charred in fire and smeared with blood. His relatives held their land directly from him. They all had the clan surname, but other men might be in the clan because they were on land the clan had taken. Macintyres, for example, were members of the Clan Campbell.

The chief held the clan land. He kept some, called *mensal land*, for himself, he gave pieces to personal attendants like the bard, the harper and the piper, and split the rest on *tack*, or lease, to his relatives, the *tacksmen*. They paid low rents and let their land to sub-tenants, who paid for it by working the tacksmen's land and looking after their cattle. This made the tacksmen sure of getting a living without having to work. They were the most important members of the clan and the chief fighting men.

Making a Living

The poorer clansmen were far worse off. It is recorded that in the Western Isles before 1600 'no labourers of the ground are permitted to steir furth of the cuntrie [leave where they lived] quhatevir their masters have ado, except only gentlemen quhilk labouris not, that the labour belonging to the teiling of the ground and the wynning of thair corns may not be left undone'.

The main job for the men was looking after their animals. They had to herd their cattle and sheep constantly to protect them from raiders and wild animals like foxes and wolves.[1] Highland cattle, called 'black cattle' but sometimes reddish or dark-brown in colour, were the Highlanders' main source of wealth. In May the herds drove them to the hill pastures for the summer. The women and girls went to live in the shielings up there, and made butter and cheese. In September drovers took many of the beasts to be sold at the Cattle Tryst at Crieff, because there was not enough feeding to keep them all through the winter. Highland cows did not give much milk, only a Scots pint [about two litres] a day, compared with over eighteen litres from a good Ayrshire cow today. Sheep, too, were milked, besides providing a little fine wool which was used to clothe the Highlanders.

Not much of the land was good for growing crops. Some pieces of land were cultivated with a wooden plough pulled by four highland ponies, and in patches higher up with a caschrom (page 60). From oats they made oatcakes and porridge, but the Highlanders, who never grew enough corn for themselves, bartered butter or cattle for grain with the Lowland farmers.

Clans nearest to the Lowlands often stole cattle and drove them home. Sometimes they levied blackmail [took money] in return for a promise to protect a farmer's cattle. A letter written by Cameron of Lochiel shows how common cattle

[1] The last wolf was killed in 1743.

raids were. His men had been accused of raiding a farm belonging to one of the Grants, but Lochiel protested, 'My men were not in your bounds, but in Murray [Moray] lands where all men take their prey.'

Weapons and Dress

Feuds between one clan and another, cattle-reiving and droving, all required the Highlander to be a fighter. His chief weapon was a basket-hilted broadsword. It left him one hand free, and he carried on his left arm a targe [shield] and in his left hand a dirk [dagger]. His round targe, covered with studded leather, had a long spike in the centre. He could use it to attack as well as defend himself. Armed like this, Highlanders in war liked to be on high ground and charge down on their enemies.

A man's main garment was the *plaid* or 'great wrap'. He wrapped it round his waist and threw the remainder over his shoulder. He could also wear it to cover the upper part of his body like a cloak. The plaid acted as a blanket as well. It could be difficult to fight in, and before an attack the Highlanders took off their plaids and charged in their shirts. Women wore self-coloured dresses of wool and linen, with a checked plaid over their shoulders. At this time no clan turned out all wearing the same tartan. In battle all the men from the same clan wore the same emblem in their bonnets. The MacDonalds of Clanranald, for example, wore heather and the Frasers sprigs of yew.

Homes

The Highland house had thick walls of stones built without cement and a thatched roof. Since he spent most of his life out

Highlanders wearing belted plaids in different ways

Inside an Orkney house early this century. Notice the two box-beds, the floor of flag stones and the fire in the middle of the floor

of doors, the Highlander thought of his house as a shelter from the rain and the cold, a shelter for both man and beast. His cow was valuable to him and occupied the byre at one end of the house. The door, often the only outside door, opened into the byre, and to reach the living quarters he passed through a lobby between two box-beds into the kitchen. There a peat-fire burned, warming the cooking-pot which hung by a chain from the rafters. If there was another 'little room' it would be separated from the kitchen only by a wooden partition.

Box-beds with heather to lie on, a few three-legged stools and a bench to sit on, these were usually the only articles of furniture. The women spun with spindles and whorls by the glint of the fire. The family sat 'round the fire' on stools or flat stones, with one for any wanderer who might want to come in.

The people lived in small settlements: there were few towns. Until 1641 most Highland trade was in the hands of the Inverness merchants. Gradually, markets and fairs were started in new burghs like Wick and Dingwall or places like Portree, where two fairs were held each year after 1693. Highland women might want ribbons, spoons, wooden plates, combs and shears, but they had little to sell in return:

a cheese or two, a little butter or some woollen cloth. For most of them, the wandering chapman or pedlar supplied all they could afford from the outside world.

King, Churches and Clans

It was always difficult to make the Highlanders obey the king's laws. When the MacGregors killed a great many of the clan Colquhoun in 1603, James VI decided to root out the whole of that clan. He hanged a dozen of them and put a price on the heads of others. They had all to take new surnames in order to stay alive.

The Bishop of Iona got the chiefs in the west to agree to the *Statutes of Iona* in 1609. They promised to stop fighting other clans and to make their men faithful members of his kind of Protestant Church, a church with bishops. The Roman Catholic Church kept its hold over other clans, like the MacDonalds, with the help of preachers who came across from Ireland. As a result, many of the Highlanders, with the notable exception of the Campbells, belonged to different churches from the one the Convenanters were fighting for in the south.

Something for You to Do

1. If you have a Highland name, you can find out about your clan, its district and tartan in *Kinsmen and Clansmen* by R. W. Munro (Johnston & Bacon). It also includes several Border names.
2. Make a diagram to show how a chief might divide up the clan land between the tacksmen, his personal attendants and other members of the clan. Put the chief at the top, the people who got their land from him below him, and the people who were given land by them at the bottom.
3. Write notes on: clan; fiery cross; shieling; blackmail.
4. *a*) In what ways is the Orkney house in the picture like the Highland homes described on pages 130–1?
   b) In what ways is it better?
5. Either draw a plan of a Highlander's house, or make a model with plasticine. Push stone chips into the plasticine walls to give a 'dry-stone' effect. Use match-boxes for box-beds and for the partition. The roof, which should lift off to show the ground-plan, can be made of plasticine or foam-rubber.

27 Life in the Burghs in the Seventeenth Century

During the seventeenth century, over a hundred new burghs of barony were founded. Many of them had been the main village on a lord's land and were given the right to hold a market. If they were good centres, they might sometimes win trade from a nearby royal burgh. From 1672, the new burghs were also given the right to trade abroad if they wished.

There were many burghs in Fife. As Sir Walter Scott's character, Andrew Fairservice, said, 'There's the Kingdom of Fife, frae Culross to the East Neuk, it's just like a great combined city, sae mony royal burghs yoked end on end.' These ports faced the Forth and traded across the North Sea.

Culross (pronounced *Cooris*) grew up beside an abbey. It became a royal burgh in 1588, and was a flourishing little port exporting coal and salt. The Civil War, and the wars with the Dutch and then the French, interrupted Scotland's trade so much that Fletcher of Saltoun was driven to declare at the end of the century that 'the Fife seaports once very prosperous are in our day little better than so many heaps of ruins.' When its coal ran out after 1700, the other industries declined and Culross fell asleep. This century the National Trust for Scotland has restored many of its old buildings, and kept alive a seventeenth-century burgh for us to see today.

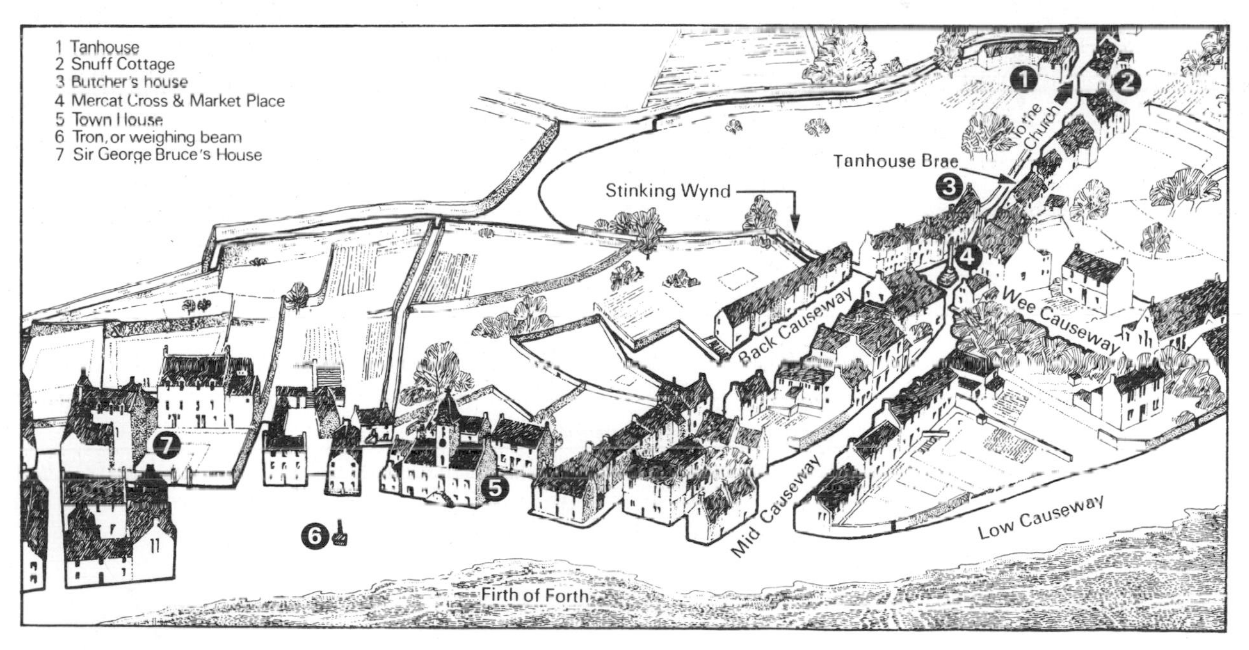

Plan of seventeenth-century Culross (the Town House tower is later)

Sir George Bruce's house,
(A Lum, B Crow-steps, C Shutters,
D Forestairs, E Cobbles)

The Busy Burgh of Culross

Visiting it now you step back in time; you are in a seventeenth-century burgh. Walk up the narrow streets and you will see that they are highest in the centre where there is a row of flat stones to walk on. Cobble stones from the beach have been laid on each side, sloping down to the gutters. The middle of the road, the 'croon of the causeway' as it is called, is the best place to walk, out of the water and rubbish. The merchants walk on the 'croon' and expect apprentices and other people to stand aside to let them pass.

The houses are close together, shielding each other from the wind. They are built of stone with low doorways and little windows. The walls of some are painted in pleasant colours and many of the gable ends have *crow-steps*, a zig-zag of stones leading up to the chimney. The masons built like this to keep the house dry where the roof meets the gable-end. 'Lums' are set in the end of the house. The roofs are bright orange tiles from Holland but some houses are still covered with thatch.

Sir George Bruce is the driving force in the burgh. He has bought up most of the salt-pans, which use up a great deal of coal. He has a coal-mine which is one of the marvels of Scotland. It has two shafts, and miners can go up or down either on land, or out in the sea. A round stone tower has been built out in the Forth, higher than the level of high tide. Down these two shafts, the miners cut through the rock into a rich seam of coal. They have made a huge tunnel, curved in the shape of an arch and high enough for a man to stand up in. Many side-cuttings branch out from it, like side-streets and closes in a town. These men cut coal, in faint candle-light, out under the sea. Water seeping through the roof makes the mine wet. Three horses (page 135) move round and round working a chain of thirty-six buckets which bring the water up to the surface and pour it back into the sea. (This mine was later flooded and wrecked in a great storm in 1625.)

Along the shore, sea-water is trapped in ponds at high tide. Some of the water evaporates in the heat of the sun. Poured into rows of flat iron pans it is heated over coal fires. Steam belches forth until all the water has boiled away. Men shovel the salt into baskets and cart them off to storehouses ready for export. Bruce's workers are now producing over ninety tonnes of salt a week.

Coal and salt, land and trade make Sir George Bruce rich. The miners and salters are his serfs. They have not become free like most townsmen and peasants. Wives and sons follow the men down the mine. No member of the family can escape to another trade. (Miners did not become free until 1799.)

Where the smiths are working, the clang of their hammers is deafening! They take a lump of hot iron and keep hammering it until they have made it flat and round. When they have joined on a handle at the side, they have made 'a guid Culross griddle' or girdle. James VI came and watched them at work in 1599 and he gave them the sole right of making girdles like these in Scotland. The mark they put on each one, the crown and the hammer, shows where it came from. Housewives at home and abroad like them for baking oatcakes and oatmeal bannocks on the fire.

Other craftsmen, too, are busy. The tanners are working on skins and leather at the top of Tanhouse Brae; the shoemakers and weavers have work to finish for next week's market at the Mercat Cross. Often we can tell by the smell where some men work, the butchers and bakers for example, but sometimes they mark their houses with the signs of their trade. A carving of a cleaver and a spring balance on a stone in the wall tell us where the Culross butcher lives. Up the hill lives the snuff-maker, who grinds tobacco into a fine powder. Many people like to sniff it up their noses. Some words above his door show his surprise at the new craze, and they might have said more:

Wha' would ha' thocht it
Noses would ha' bocht it.

How the water was pumped out of Sir George Bruce's coal-mine

A man is being hustled up the steps of the Town House. A red-faced man is complaining, 'I sold him a fine pair of breeks last week and he hasn't paid me a penny.'

'Save your breath for the Council,' commands the bailie who made the arrest. The case is heard by the Council and the man, found guilty, is locked in the debtor's room. If he had been guilty of any other crime he would have been put in the prison below the council chamber. When he does not come out along with the Council, the people know that this is another case of a man who has not paid his debts.

Not far from the Town House is Sir George Bruce's home, the finest in Culross (page 134). He just calls it 'The Collier's House' but it shows that he has money to spend. It is a big house, which has doubled in size during his lifetime. An old mason is busy chiselling 'S.G.B.', the initials for Sir George Bruce, on a stone for the top of a dormer window. Glaziers are preparing lattice windows, fitting the diamond-shaped glass together with strips of lead. The windows are not made to open and shut, but below the glass part of each window are two little doors or shutters which open to let in the air. All the bedrooms are lined with the finest Baltic pine and painted with bright patterns and pictures. We hear that Sir George Bruce plans to employ an artist to paint more Biblical scenes on the ceilings.

Down in the harbour, men are loading cartloads of coals on board ships bound for ports in Holland, Germany and the Baltic. A carter has just brought linen yarn and bales of cloth from Dunfermline, and will carry back timber just unloaded from Norway.

Tools of the butcher's trade, carved on his tombstone in Culross cemetery

Traders and Manufacturers

On the whole, the main cargoes Scottish traders sent abroad were skins and hides, as well as wool, linen and woollen cloth, salt herrings and salmon. Gradually coal was becoming the most popular export to the Netherlands and many Dutch ships came over to collect it. In the past, the Scots had sent most of their goods to the Netherlands, especially the port of Campvere where they were given more freedom to trade than they had with England. Many Scottish families settled in Campvere. There was also a Scottish lodging-house where Scottish merchants on a visit would stay, and they could worship in their own church. It was Thomas Cunningham, a merchant in Campvere, who sent to Scotland the weapons the Covenanters needed in the Civil War. As Scottish merchants began to send more ships to trade with ports on the Baltic, such as Stockholm and Danzig, others went out to live there or in towns in Poland.

Merchants in different Scottish burghs had their ups and downs in trade. The fishing ports of Fife sold fewer fish in Holland, while other ports like Culross sent out more coal and salt. In the west, Glasgow men started new industries and were building up their trade, especially to Ireland, and risking a smuggling trip now and then to America. Edinburgh was still by far the richest town: into its port of Leith came one-third of all the goods imported into Scotland, including most of the wine.

In the 1680s Parliament did its best to help new Scottish firms to make things in Scotland, such as sugar, soap, gunpowder and pottery, as well as cloth. To let Scottish cloth-makers have the home market to themselves, it passed an act to stop all kinds of cloth coming in from abroad. Near Haddington, the New Mills Company started to make fine cloth on a large scale. The place was a hive of industry for several years, but it could not make enough cloth for the whole of Scotland. After the Union of 1707 English merchants could again send good quality cloth north free of duty. The New Mills could not sell theirs so cheaply and before long they had to close down.

Something for You to Do

1. *a*) West or east, which side of Scotland had most of the foreign trade in the seventeenth century, and why?
   b) Why did trade with Europe decay later in the century?
2. Make a list, or a set of drawings, of the features of a house in a seventeenth-century burgh. There may be some houses near you which are of this period, e.g. Gladstone's Land and many others in the Royal Mile in Edinburgh, and Provand's Lordship in Glasgow. Look out for houses with small windows, crow-stepped gables, etc.
3. What powers did a town council have in the seventeenth century which a district council in the last quarter of the twentieth century does not?
4. If you live in a town which is as old as Culross, try to reconstruct what it must have been like at this time. (Houses, streets, crafts, markets, the council, crimes, punishments may be interesting topics.)
5. Kathleen Fidler's novel, *Escape in Darkness*, describes the wreck of Sir George Bruce's coal-mine at Culross.

28 The Union of Scotland and England

In 1690, the Scottish Parliament became free and could begin to do things for the benefit of the Scottish people, even if they were not in the best interests of England.

The Scots had one constant grudge against the English. Compared with England, Scotland was poor with no colonies and little trade. In spite of the Union of the Crowns, she was considered by England to be a foreign country and could not trade with England or the English colonies without paying duties. At this time countries tried to produce all the goods they needed for themselves, and kept out foreign goods by putting on heavy duties. If they had colonies abroad, they kept all the trade with them for themselves.

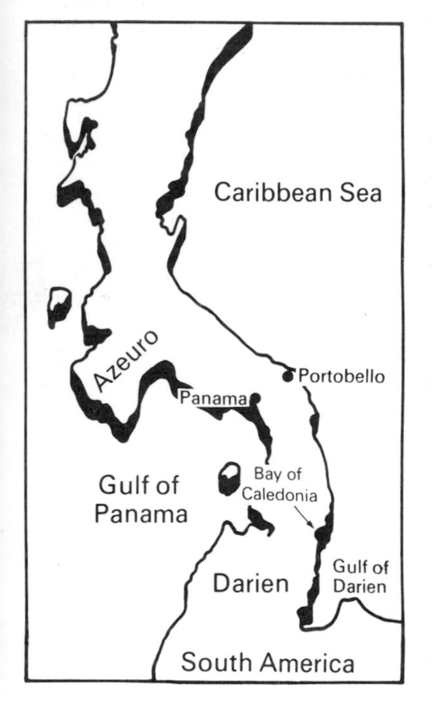

The Darien Scheme

Scotland's foreign trade was drying up and some merchants decided to start a colony of their own. In 1695 they formed a company, 'The Company of Scotland Trading to Africa and the Indies', and were given the right to trade between Scotland and America, Africa and Asia for thirty-one years. William Paterson had a plan, and they thought he ought to know all about making money, as he had just helped to found the Bank of England. A great many landowners and merchants invested their savings, £150 000 in all, in the new venture. *Darien*, on the narrow strip of land joining North and South America, was the place Paterson chose for this great centre of buying and selling by the Scots.

Paterson had not considered all the problems of setting up a colony there: the heat, malaria, the need to break in the land for crops, or the Spaniards who claimed that the land was theirs. Not enough thought was given to what people would want to buy there, and there was little demand for the heavy cloths, stockings and wigs they took out. The Spaniards who had settled in Central America did not want to share their trade with any other country. When the Scots turned to the English in Jamaica for help, they were astounded when none was given. But why should the English help Scotsmen to start a colony which would be competing with their own traders? This Scottish scheme also interfered with William III's plans to keep Spain friendly.

3d some of our men were sent ashore to clear ground for ye rest
4 these were releived and ours sent ashore
5 All our souldiers & oficers yt were in health went ashore to work
6 the printers boy dyed
8th All our sick men were carried ashore, At night one of our Gen
: lemen named Ja: Clerk dyed
9th one mr fenner servt to mr Paterson dyed
12 Mr Patersons Lady dyed
17th John Sim who was stewart to ye Captn dyed
19th Mr Adam Scot our minister dyed
21 one of our midshipmen named Andrew Hamilton dyed
24 our Councellors gave orders yt the Endeavour should be sent
home for Scotland, but countermanded since, because every day
we were told by the Indians yt ye Spaniards are coming to fight
against us. Here I shal make ane end of my Journall.

Events of November 1698 from the journal Colin Campbell kept on his voyage to Darien on board the *Unicorn*

The Darien Scheme was a dismal failure. Hundreds of settlers lost their lives and all the money was gone. In their misery the Scots put the blame not on their mistakes, but on the king and the English merchants. The Union of the Crowns was never nearer to breaking point.

The Massacre of Glencoe

The Highlanders already had reason to hate the king. Their chiefs had been made to swear an oath of loyalty to William and Mary. The deadline was 31st December 1691. To some of the chiefs, it was a matter of honour to be slow in taking the oath. MacIan, chief of the MacDonalds of Glencoe, reported in time to the commander of the troops at Fort William, who told him that he should have gone to Inveraray to take the oath before the sheriff. MacIan was old, the weather was miserable, and he struggled through the snow to Inveraray. He had to wait until the sheriff arrived, and he took the oath on the 6th January 1692. The sheriff seemed satisfied, and the old chief thought his duty done.

Sir John Dalrymple, the Master of Stair, who had the chief power in Scotland at the time, was delighted when he heard that MacIan had been late. Here was a chance to make an example of a small clan. A hundred and twenty soldiers, led by Campbell of Glenlyon, a deadly enemy of the MacDonalds, arrived in the glen. They came in peace, they said, and were kindly treated at the tables and firesides of the MacDonalds for nearly a fortnight. Before light one

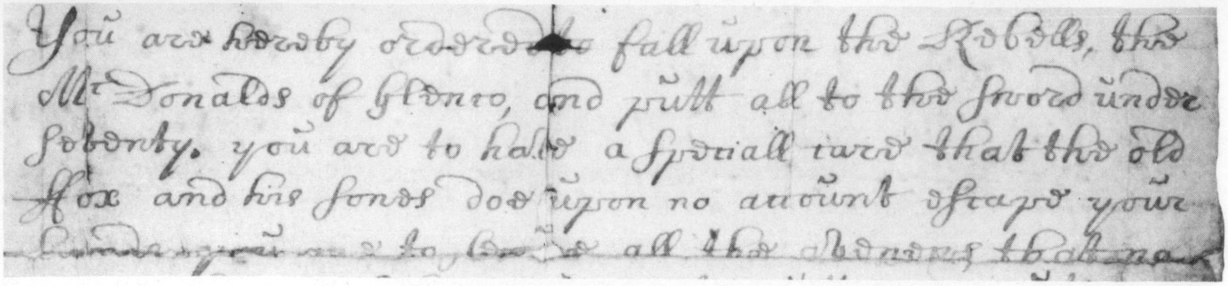
You are hereby ordered to fall upon the Rebells, the McDonalds of Glenco, and putt all to the sword under sebenty. you are to have a speciall care that the old fox and his sones doe upon no account escape your

Order to Campbell of Glenlyon ten days after his troops arrived in Glencoe:
'You are hereby ordered to fall upon the rebels, the MacDonalds of Glencoe, and put all to the sword under seventy. You are to have a special care that the old fox and his sons do upon no account escape your hands.'

February morning, they struck. The chief was shot in his bed, and nearly forty men, women and children were put to the sword, while others struggled through the snow to safety among the Stewarts of Appin.

Many questions about the massacre were left unanswered. Who was to blame? Was it Dalrymple, the Master of Stair? Was he the planner or the faithful royal servant? Was it the king? He signed the order, but did he understand what was to happen? One thing is certain: this action turned the Highlanders against 'Dutch William' and his government.

'The Ill Years'

From 1695 onwards the crops failed, and the people called that time 'the seven ill years'. Harvests were so late that harvesting was still going on in January. Food was dear, and many people died from cold and hunger. An eye-witness tells us, 'I have seen when meal was all sold in markets, women clapping their hands and tearing the clothes off their heads, crying "How shall we go home and see our children die in hunger? They have got no meat these two days and we have nothing to give them."'

The tragedies of Glencoe, Darien and 'the ill years', made the Scots feel sorry for themselves. They thought, 'Would it not be better to break away from England and become a separate nation again?' When Britain was at war with France in Queen Anne's reign, the English feared that the Scots might choose a king of their own and take France's side. They decided to allow the Scots to have free trade, if they would agree to one Parliament for the whole of Britain.

The Act of Union

In 1707 the Union of the Parliaments, took place. It meant the end of the old Scottish Parliament, where lords, lairds and burgesses had all sat in the same House where, as Andrew Fairservice said in *Rob Roy*, 'they didna need to hae the same blethers twice ower'. Forty-five Members of Parliament were to represent Scotland in the British House of Commons, and the Scottish lords were to choose sixteen of their number to sit in the House of Lords.

Scottish merchants were free to trade with England and the English colonies. At first, Scottish goods could not compare with English ones, but increasing numbers of cattle were driven into England and sold. The cattle trade brought in money, some of which helped to improve farming and the linen industry. Glasgow merchants could now openly import tobacco from Virginia, and the town prospered.

Both countries were to use the same coins, weights and measures, and their Union was marked by a new flag, putting together the crosses of St George and St Andrew. They agreed that the Protestant house of Hanover would succeed to the throne on the death of Queen Anne, but in religion and law Scotland clung to her old ways. The Kirk remained the established Church in Scotland. Her system of law was kept although it was different from English law. All members of an English jury, for example, had until recently to agree, whereas in Scotland a majority verdict was enough. A prisoner in England may be either 'guilty' or 'not guilty' but in Scotland a third verdict of 'not proven' [proved] is possible.

The two peoples united to form one country, Great Britain, and their political history as separate countries came to an end. After 1707, their politics and relations with other countries became the subject-matter of British history. This does not mean that the Scottish nation ceased to exist. Scotland has its own local dialects, songs, dances, stories, customs and traditions – everything that makes up Scottish culture and makes us feel 'Scottish'. This feeling lives on. If you watch an international football or rugby match you will soon realise that the feeling of Scottish people for their team, and therefore their country is still strong.

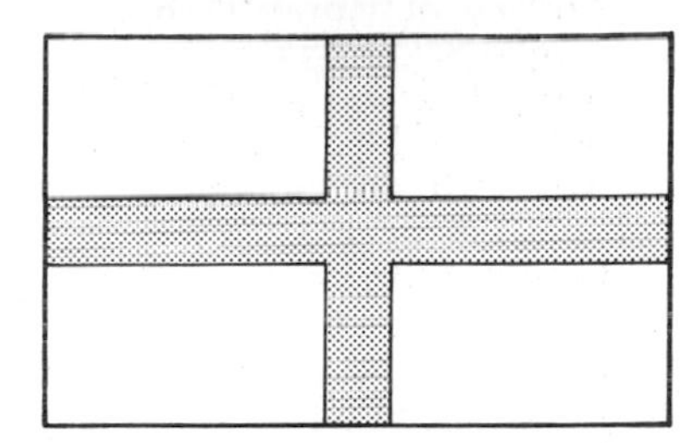

Saltire of St Andrew, cross of St George and the Union flag of 1707

Something for You to Do

1. Write an account of the Massacre of Glencoe as if you had been an eye-witness.
2. What do you learn from Colin Campbell's journal on page 139 about people's health and why the Darien plan failed?
3. Copy out the main terms of the Act of Union. Add the date, and the name of the monarch who signed it.
4. Discuss in class: has Scotland benefited by union with England?
5. Complete your time chart.

Index

(*Italics signify names of battles*)

TIME CHART

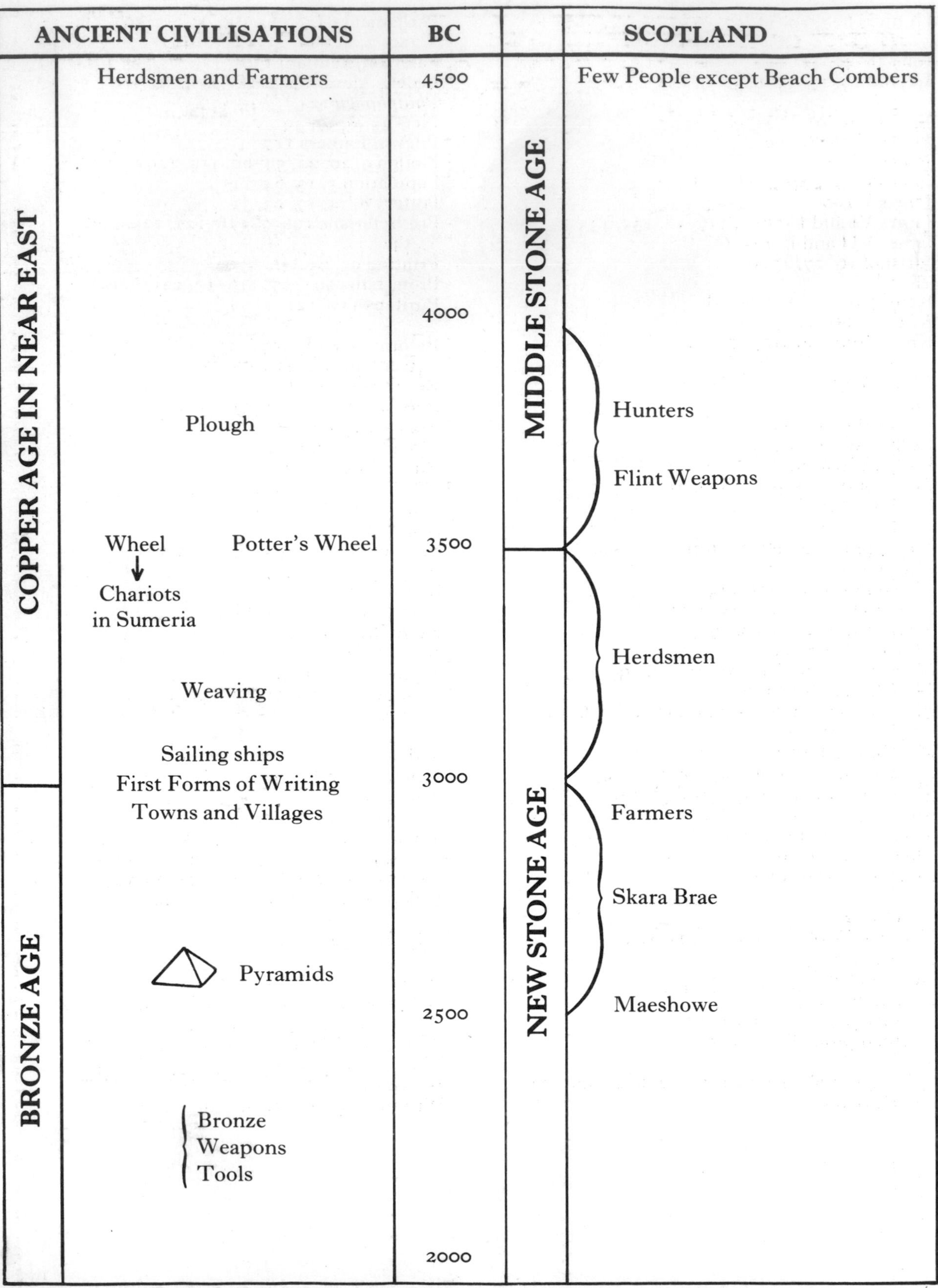
ANCIENT CIVILISATIONS
BC
SCOTLAND
COPPER AGE IN NEAR EAST
BRONZE AGE
Herdsmen and Farmers
4500
Few People except Beach Combers
MIDDLE STONE AGE
4000
Plough
Hunters
Flint Weapons
Wheel
Chariots
in Sumeria
Potter's Wheel
3500
Herdsmen
Weaving
Sailing ships
First Forms of Writing
Towns and Villages
3000
NEW STONE AGE
Farmers
Skara Brae
Pyramids
2500
Maeshowe
Bronze
Weapons
Tools
2000